Martin Luther King, Jr.

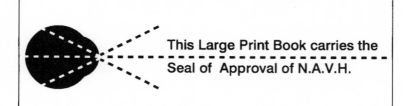

This Large Print Book carries the
Seal of Approval of N.A.V.H.

Martin Luther King, Jr.

Marshall Frady

Thorndike Press • Waterville, Maine

Published in 2002 by arrangement with Viking Penguin, a member of Penguin Putnam, Inc.

Thorndike Press Large Print Biography Series.

The tree indicium is a trademark of Thorndike Press.

The text of this Large Print edition is unabridged. Other aspects of the book may vary from the original edition.

Set in 16 pt. Plantin by Myrna S. Raven.

Printed in the United States on permanent paper.

Library of Congress Cataloging-in-Publication Data

Frady, Marshall.
    Martin Luther King, Jr. / Marshall Frady.
      p. cm.
    ISBN 0-7862-3884-4 (lg. print : hc : alk. paper)
  1. King, Martin Luther, Jr., 1929–1968. 2. African Americans
  — Biography. 3. Civil rights workers — United States —
Biography. 4. Baptists — United States — Clergy — Biography.
5. African Americans — Civil rights — History — 20th century.
6. Large type books. I. Title.
E185.97.K5 F695 2002
323'.092—dc21
[B]   2001056319

For my father
Joseph Yates Frady
Preacher of the gospel for seventy years

Contents

Introduction

Almost a geological age ago, it seems now —
that great moral saga of belief and violence
that unfolded in the musky deeps of the
South during the civil rights movement of the
fifties and sixties. It's hard to remember at
this remove of years how profoundly the
South then was like another country within
the United States. Locked into its own massive apartheid system, implacably enforced
by legal and political authorities across the
whole spectrum of its social life, it really had
more in common with the South Africa of
that day than the rest of the nation. At the
same time, the South seemed a region that
belonged to some older, more primal and
guttural script about the human situation,
tribal, stark, fatal, that was wholly outside the
general American sensibility of rationality
and optimism. Even so, it had fallen the lot of
the South, formed by slavery and its camou-
flaged sequel of segregation, to serve as the
crucible for the whole nation's periodic
struggles of conscience over its own endemic
and pervasive racial malaise. As early as Jefferson, the recognition was already gathering

that the only fundamental and intractable crisis this Republic finally faced was that of racial schism — that the American political adventure, conceived in such brave hope and largeness of idea, may have also held from its very inception, when the first black man in chains set his foot on the continent's shores, the seeds of its undoing. Indeed, that aboriginal crime has been with us, one way or another, ever since. And it was the South, living more directly and intimately in that crime than anywhere else, that seemed appointed the violent ceremonial ground for America's intermittent travails to purge itself of that primeval shame and guilt.

The civil rights movement became the nation's latest attempt to perform in the South an exorcising of its original sin, and it turned out our most epic moral drama since the Civil War itself. What was taking place for those few passionate years was a kind of high lyricism of the human spirit, played out in the unlikely stage set of bleak little cities and musty towns marooned out in the sun-shimmering backlands of the South. And for its duration, the South itself seemed to pass into a theater of the surreal. Over its countrysides could be found an exotic visitation of gentle young earnest evangels from the far winters of the North and the mild

Eden of California, having brought down with them radical humanist fervors from Harvard seminars and all-night discussions in back of Berkeley bookstores, and now damp and tallow-pale in the brutal glare of Mississippi and south Georgia, they had about them a bespectacled, vegetarian, somehow sweetly lost and fugitive quality. With them were the brimstone-eyed young black circuit riders of the movement, Caribbean plantation hats rakishly tilted low over their faces and red bandannas tucked in the top of deerskin boots, dusting from town to town in ramshackle station wagons and muddy coupes, always furiously, manically, inexhaustibly talking. . . . They were days delirious with belief.

It was while I was working one summer in the mid-sixties as an apprentice correspondent in the Atlanta bureau of *Newsweek* — still a raw young provincial just emerged out of a Southern small-town upbringing — that I was lobbed abruptly into the heats and tumults of that immense folk morality play. One smoldering night in a little Alabama town, I found myself standing in the back of a shoebox tabernacle crammed with a congregation of black maids, janitors, beauticians, schoolteachers — all the windows open to the hot ripe night outside and

11

cardboard fans advertising *Peoples Funeral Association* fluttering over the packed ranks of glistening faces — as a local preacher, a heavy, sweat-washed man just released from jail that afternoon, led them through one of those mightily swooping hymns of the movement: *O freedom! O freedom! O freedom over me, over me. . . .* I stepped outside to stand for a moment in the dark under a chinaberry tree, suddenly a bit woozy, and lighted a cigarette with trembling fingers. And with those voices in the church surging on in the night — *And before I'll be a slave, I'll be buried in my grave, and go home to my Lord and be free* — I still distinctly remember the prickling that shivered over my hide, and blurting aloud, "Good God." Such moments were a kind of Damascus Road experience in the lives of more reporters than me.

And it would all converge repeatedly into the same, almost ritualistic scene: demonstrators brimming out of a town's black neighborhood and swelling down the plain little main street with a vast clapping and low cavernous choiring — *Ain't gon' let nobody turn me 'round, turn me 'round* — the marchers moving on toward a courthouse square bristling with white deputies and state troopers waiting with shotguns and billy clubs, their faces blank and flat as nickel coins, chewing small wads of gum with only a faint stirring of their jaws. And when the two met, it seemed with the ceremonious deliberation of a dream, coming together in a strangely slow-motion collision of floundering bodies, howls and shouts, thumping clubs, a few screams. . . .

In time, of course, that passion play transpiring in the South was assimilated, without pause or intermission, by the more expansive and complex national anguish of Vietnam — while the South's racial duress also spanned out over the rest of the country, where it became more diffused and abstract, the saints and villains losing their old palpable simplicity, as the South itself meanwhile receded into the more sedate preoccupation of mutating into some regional version of the San Fernando Valley. Now, all the angers and urgencies of those years of the civil rights movement seem curiously remote, dwindled, archaic, *quaint*. But the partisans and journalists who passed through that distant time still tend to look back on it something like Lincoln Brigade veterans wistful for the bright days of Spain in '38. Goodness and courage and evil and tragedy all had, for that brief season, a marvelously simple and immediate clarity. The very air seemed vivid then with some fever of superreality. That once, at least, breath truly hit the bottom of the lungs. It was a time of an ultra-aliveness that few were ever to know again.

That moral pageantry playing over the South was all an amplification of what had begun at first obscurely, almost by happenstance, with a bus segregation protest back in 1955 in the winter glooms of Montgomery, Alabama. But the solemn young black minister reluctantly impressed into its leadership, Martin Luther King, Jr., who had remained at the center of its expanding ramifications afterward, was, when I first encountered him in St. Augustine in 1964, a startlingly unprepossessing figure — a short, chunky man, with a manner of unremitting and ponderous gravity in his deacon-sober suits. His round face, black as asphalt, wore a bland gaze of almost Oriental impassiveness, an improbable bourgeois placidness — yet with, I still remember, almost meltingly sweet eyes. But on the whole, he could have been a comfortably prosperous funeral home director, or merely what among other things he indeed was, the Baptist preacher of a big-city church. However surprisingly unheroic his appearance, though, the transfiguration of the South effected in the course of his apostleship — the momentous Black Awakening of a long subject and debased people, their eventual political ascendancy, the widely common public culture now of whites and blacks there — was by almost any measure epochal. And the legacy of racial amity that, perhaps even more astonishingly, followed that transformation would quite likely have been impossible without King's stubbornly persevering, nonviolent gospel metaphysic of redemptive understanding and forgiveness and even sorrow for one's very brutalizers. As he once bayed out, mouth thrown wide in a roar of power from the back of his thick-packed neck, when marchers were facing the dogs and clubs and fire hoses of Birmingham: "We will meet the forces of hate with the power of love. . . . We must say to our white brothers all over the South, We will match your capacity to inflict suffering with our capacity to endure suffering. . . . Bomb our homes and we will still love you. . . . We will so appeal to your heart and conscience that we will win you in the process."

But before long, King's moral vision had impelled him beyond the South into a mission, even more formidable and in the end tragic, as prophet to the whole national community at America's Augustan noon of pride and power. His evangelism against the primal Cain act of racism — its denial of a natural connection to other human beings, reducing them to objects, which then allows any manner of violence against them — inexorably evolved into an evangelism against what he saw as the moral coma of the country's whole corporate, technological order: its loud and vicious void of materialism, its isolation of individuals from each other, its technician's detachment from the human effects of its interests and policies, and the measureless vandalism this new kind of high-tech barbarism was visiting not only on the life of America, but elsewhere in the world, most luridly at that time in Vietnam. In effect, he came to pit himself against his entire age. Toward the end, he committed himself to a grand social offensive of not only blacks but Hispanics, Native Americans, poor whites, all the dispossessed and discarded and forgotten of American society, to radically reorder the values and power system of the whole nation: he had wound up, as J. Edgar Hoover was not far wrong in fuming, the most subversive man in America. But that was the final, huge, Gandhian ambition that came to consume him: through the same nonviolent mass confrontations that had remade the South, to do nothing less than re-create and re-deem America itself. In that sense, he was really just beginning when, only some twelve years after Montgomery, he wandered out to his motel room balcony in Memphis that mild April dusk in 1968.

Over the years since then, ironically, King has passed into the cloudy shimmers of a pop beatification, commemorated with parades, memorial concerts, schools and streets and parks named for him, his birthday a national holiday, his image on postage stamps. But in the process, a benignly nebulous amnesia has settled over how in fact tenuous, fitful, and uncertain was his progress through those years from Montgomery to Memphis, and the final, truly revolutionary implications of his message. More, the man himself has been abstracted out of his swelteringly convoluted actuality into a kind of weightless and reverently laminated effigy of who he was. To hallow a figure is almost always to hollow him. And the truth is, King was always a far more excruciatingly complex soul than the subsequent flattenings effected by his mass sanctification. As one of his biographers,

David L. Lewis, put it, in "the nation's can-
onization of Martin King . . . we have
sought to remember him by forgetting
him."

Four years before Memphis, there was
one glowering summer night in Florida's
little moss-hung antique of a city, St. Augustine, where King had mounted a series of
demonstrations that I was sent down by
Newsweek to cover — night marches that
proceeded with a hymning of freedom songs
from the black quarter of town to the town
square, once a slave market, where they
would be met with an engulfing violence
from the whites who had been steadily
sifting in from the surrounding palmetto
flatlands. After those nightly melees on the
square, the reporters there — many of them
veterans by now of racial uproars all the way
back to the Autherine Lucy riots at the University of Alabama of 1956 — would quickly
retreat to their motel rooms to get swiftly,
slammingly drunk. But then came one particular Walpurgis Night of mayhem on the
square — a storm of swinging baseball bats
and trace chains and shrieked rebel yells,
through which the black marchers made
their way with a mute, unbelieving terror
and stumbling frantic urgency, in a long
leaning line battered back and forth like a

18

canebrake in a wild wind, and at last breaking apart altogether, marchers scattering back for the refuge of the black section. Following them there, through several passing scuffles of my own, I happened to glimpse, in the shadows of a front porch, all by himself and apparently unnoticed by anyone else, King standing in his shirt-sleeves, his hands on his hips, absolutely motionless as he watched the marchers straggling past him in the dark, bleeding, clothes torn, sobs and wails now welling up everywhere around him — and on his face a look of stricken astonishment.

Later that night, I found him sitting behind drawn blinds in the low-lit front parlor of another house, holding a glass of ice water with a paper napkin wrapped around the bottom. He said in a thick murmur, "You question — yes, when things happen like this tonight, you question sometimes — *What are we doing to these people? . . .*" Even so, when earlier that evening he had been watching that retreat from the square staggering past him, I had seen on his face not only shock at what had befallen these people acting on his exhortations, but also it seemed a kind of wonder and fascination at this collision precipitated by his moral vision's dramaturgy of good and evil — and at the same time, some deeper horror at that very captivation in himself.

"I am a troubled soul," King admitted more than once. Indeed, long before Memphis, he had come to dwell in a private Gethsemane of guilt over not only the cost of his mission on his people, but what he felt were his own personal betrayals of his high public meaning. Always haunted by a reverence for the austere and ascetic, he attempted to maintain a modesty in his own circumstances, confining himself to a meager salary, a small rented frame house in a humble neighborhood, an old car, plain dark suits. Yet those suits were often silk, as were the pajamas he would have brought to him whenever he could for his stays in jail. He remained discreetly but resistlessly infatuated with the glamours of importance: limousine transport to imperial hotel suites, the company of the wealthy and eminent. Neither was he innocent of a certain fretful pride in his appearance, in his intellectual heft, his historical import, which prompted journalist David Halberstam once to note that "the average reporter . . . suspects King's vanity." In truth, King was surrounded during his days by accusations, not just from antagonists, but from many journalists and occasionally close associates, of a breathtaking pompousness, a brazen and sometimes craven opportunism, as well as a forlorn ineptness in administering his organization, the Southern Christian Leadership Conference, even a troubling casualness in its financial accountings.

Also, King would frequently deplore "the evils of sensuality," declaring in one sermon, "Each of us is two selves. And the great burden of life is always to keep that higher self in command. Don't let the lower self take over." But not long after his death began the ripple of reports about his extramarital amatory disportings. They were almost impossible to believe at first, simply because they seemed so wildly at variance, just did not rhyme, with his unrelenting public demeanor of gravitas. But as the reports continued to accumulate of lickerish rompings in hotel rooms, multiple humid affairs, they finally became too plentiful from too many responsible sources to be reasonably doubted. Some apologists at first suggested that it was simply of a piece with the ardent nature of a man unable to apply economies to his passions. But more than that, in King's lapses into that "lower self" he so often decried, one sensed an extraordinarily harrowed man — caught in the almost insupportable strain of having to sustain the high spirituality of his mass moral struggle, while living increasingly in a daily expectation of death — intermittently resorting to releases into sweetly obliterating riots of the flesh. He seemed thus to move through some endlessly recycling alternation between the transcendently spiritual and the convulsively carnal. And with King's exorbitant propensity for guilt, it was as if all such lapses into a lesser self violating the high nobility of his public mission could be expiated only by surrendering himself to a readiness to die for it — a fatal expectation with him, in fact, from his beginnings in Montgomery. In a sense, then, the outer turbulence attending King's movement was all along matched by an unseen, equally turbulent struggle within King himself.

But such baser aspects in the Promethean moral protagonists in history — Gandhi himself, by the later testimony of associates, could be exquisitely vindictive, curtly cold to family and others close to him personally, with "an insatiable love of power and implacability in its pursuit" — hardly diminish the splendor of such figures. Rather, they lend them a far grander human meaning than their eventual, depthless pop exaltations. But we have not yet learned to accommodate in our understanding of such figures what the ancient seers, Sophocles and the King David chronicler and Shakespeare and Cervantes, knew — that while evil can wear the most civil and sensible and respectably rectitudinous demeanor, good can seem blunderous and uncertain, shockingly wayward, woefully flawed, like one of Graham Greene's dissolute, shabby, God-haunted saints. And what the full-bodied reality of King should finally tell us, beyond all the awe and celebration of him, is how mysteriously mixed, in what torturously complicated forms, our moral heroes — our prophets — actually come to us.

Out of Egypt

King's father always presented a more imposing figure, in a way, than his eldest son ever would. A strapping, boomingly assertive man, commandingly erect and chesty, Martin Luther King, Sr. — later to be known as "Daddy King" — was the bluffly autocratic preacher at Atlanta's Ebenezer Baptist Church, who liked to advertise how, at one congregational meeting, he had quelled an obstreperous member by threatening to collapse a chair over his head. Raised a sharecropper's son in south Georgia, called then Mike, he was burly enough at fourteen to grapple his drunken father away from beating his mother. After the ferocious fight that ensued, his mother, fearing that Mike or his father would sooner or later kill the other, made her son flee to Atlanta. Mike King arrived in the alien clamors of that city, as he later allowed, "smelling like a mule," but full of a barging industriousness: belatedly plowing his way through high school classes, he was preaching at two country churches by the time he was twenty.

He had also begun to pay court to the

daughter of the minister then at Ebenezer, A. D. Williams, himself a slave preacher's son who had diligently made his way up to become one of the presiding worthies of Atlanta's black community. Alberta was the Williamses' only child, a plain, thick, shy girl, almost twenty, who played the organ at her father's services, and Mike King was the first suitor ever to seriously approach her. After a six-year courtship of the most filigreed formality, they were finally married on Thanksgiving Day of 1926 and lived in the Williamses' commodious Victorian house. In due time, Mike King would also assume Williams's pulpit at Ebenezer.

Sixteen months after the birth of a daughter, their first son was delivered, in their bedroom, on January 15, 1929, and named Michael after his father. Only when "Little Mike" was five would the elder King change both their names to Martin Luther, thereby depositing one of the first heavy loads of expectation, both his own and history's, on the slight shoulders of his eldest boy. Sixteen months after Little Mike's birth, another son was born, named A.D. after Alberta's father and also to become a preacher, but who was to prove for most of his life a flounderingly troubled spirit.

Martin was a small, somewhat tubby

child, with a plump face and watchful, darkly glistening "almond-shaped eyes," by one description. Reared under his father's fierce protectiveness in a comfortably middle-class family, amid the extravagant attentions of his father's congregation, he early came by a sense of being at the privileged center of the world around him. Enclosed by a city not unfamiliar with the sulfurs of racist acrimony and violence common to the South at that time, Atlanta's black community yet had, with its complex of universities and flourishing black enterprises, its own order of bourgeois gentility. One of its main thoroughfares, Auburn Avenue, up a rise from which both Ebenezer and the King house were located, was a lively gallery of cafés, lawyers' offices, small businesses, nightspots, that had come to be known as "Sweet Auburn." Within the benign insulations of this world, Martin grew up a singularly favored boy, evidencing an early oversize appetite for both soul food and opera, for strenuous bouts of wrestling and playing "Moonlight Sonata" on the piano. Though his schoolwork tended to be somewhat haphazard, with an indifference to spelling and grammar that was to persist for the rest of his life, he had a precociously restless intelligence — and was not unaware of it himself. He notified his mother, after hearing the splendiferous rhetoric of a visiting preacher one Sunday, "Someday I'm going to have me some big words like that." Before too long, he would be startling his teachers by producing such locutions as, to a casual query about how he was doing, "Cogitating with the cosmic universe, I surmise that my physical equilibrium is organically quiescent." He also took to employing this volubility to extricate himself from fights. On the whole, he seemed to revel in the widening discovery of his gifts, his possibilities.

His father, however, was not so impressed with those nimble facilities of his son that he did not regularly administer, for his rowdier impulses, rigorous whippings. A neighbor would later report hearing the senior King, in the middle of one such walloping, whooping to Martin that "he would make something of him even if he had to beat him to death." To be sure, the elder King's wrath fell on both his sons impartially, and Martin's younger brother, A.D., never seemed able, even when a man, to free himself from their father's baleful intimidation. Martin himself would later gamely profess that "whippings must not be so bad, for I received them until I was fifteen." Even when not applied by hand or strap, his father's disciplines could still be fearsome. After catching Martin, in his teens, cavorting with girls at a YMCA dance, the senior King compelled him to perform the mortifying exercise of apologizing personally before Ebenezer's congregation. Yet even as a small boy, Martin seemed to receive all these scourgings with some strange, willed remove of resignation. "He was the most peculiar child whenever you whipped him," Daddy King would later allow himself to marvel. "He'd stand there, and the tears would run down, and he'd never cry."

Indeed, his teachers and others soon noted he was frequently given to a withdrawn moodiness. No doubt part of it was that, from his first memories, he had felt himself carrying the oppressive weight of his father's unappealable assumption that he would eventually join him in the pastorship of Ebenezer. But beyond that, if Martin had grown up sensing himself at the blessed center of the world around him, at the same time he seemed to feel at the center of responsibility for what happened in it. He early showed an inordinate compulsion to take on himself great cargoes of guilt — which impelled him, twice before he was thirteen, to bizarre gestures of suicide, both

times leaping out of a window over an unbearable grief about his grandmother,
whose most cherished grandchild he always
knew he was. The second time, having
slipped away one Sunday to watch a downtown parade, he instantly supposed that this
little delinquency accounted for his grandmother's death by heart attack that afternoon, and he flung himself with sobbing
abandon out of the second-floor window of
the house.

For a child so excruciatingly serious,
while so bountifully gifted and filled with an
ambitious eagerness for life, the chill discovery that, despite growing up an auspicious young prince in the black community,
he actually belonged to a lesser caste in the
larger white order around him — the immemorial trauma for African Americans in the
South then — was particularly devastating.
When he was six, a white friend of his childhood suddenly vanished into his own
school, forbidden to play with him any
longer. Once, in a downtown department
store, he was slapped by a white matron who
shrilled, "The little nigger stepped on my
foot." The flashes of proud and unafraid
protest he happened to witness in his father
at such racial affronts were not lost on him:
once, when the senior King was stopped by

a traffic policeman who addressed him as "boy," he pointed to Martin on the seat beside him and snapped, "That's a boy. I'm a man." Another time, he stalked out of a store with Martin when a shoe clerk insisted they move to the rear to be served, rumbling, "We'll either buy shoes sitting here or won't buy any shoes at all." In summer jobs at a mattress company and the Railway Express, Martin was depressed by the debasement of black employees, and quit at the Railway Express when a white superintendent kept calling him "nigger." In time, he was to venture with several other students out of Atlanta for a summer of working in the zestily interracial company of a tobacco farm in Connecticut. But that bracing experience only made more insufferable such incidents as, when returning by bus with his teacher from a high school oratorical contest in a south Georgia town, where Martin had delivered to much acclaim a speech titled "The Negro and the Constitution," the bus driver demanded they give up their seats when more white passengers boarded, and the two of them had to stand the ninety miles back to Atlanta — a memory surely lingering in what was to happen some fourteen years later in Montgomery.

From those initial humiliations, King

later recounted, "I was determined to hate every white person." It was a blank animus not really dispelled until his involvement with several integrated campus groups during his college years. But it all left in him that stilted reserve he would always maintain in public, and especially in the presence of whites — as if careful to present, against the white Southerner's coarse image of blacks that had visited those early outrages on him, an unfaltering comportment of what Matthew Arnold termed "high seriousness."

Partly for the same reason, he developed by his teens a fastidious aversion to the lusty religious style in his father's church — the whoops, the clapping, the sweats, the transports. Soon, though still inescapably weighted with his father's dynastic pastoral expectations — or precisely because of that — he entered into proud adolescent apostasies about the intellectual respectability of his father's fundamentalist religion, scandalizing his Sunday school class once by denying the literal bodily resurrection of Jesus. Eventually, of course, his power to move multitudes would come largely from having grown up in the scriptural dramaturgies and oratorical raptures of those church services at Ebenezer. But at the time, "it embar-

31

rassed me," King later admitted. In that distaste lurked perhaps a certain developing preciousness of self-regard. But more, it intimated a revulsion, a wariness about belonging in any way to white Southerners' minstrel caricature of blacks as loud, slovenly, childishly emotional, witless of discipline and dignity. His horror of being captured in that fundamentally annihilating image, effacing all he actually was, accounted not a little for the relentlessly staid public manner, the neat dark suits, the almost lugubrious decorums of deportment he was to assume for the rest of his life.

Still, by the testimony of one friend from those beginning years, "he loved to party, he loved to enjoy life." By the time he entered Atlanta's Morehouse College — having skipped grades to graduate from high school at fifteen — he had become something of a swell, disposed to snazzy sports jackets, flaring-brimmed hats, snappy two-toned shoes, coming by the nickname of "Tweed" for the donnish tweed suits he particularly liked to affect. Just as fancy — despite his short and relatively homely person — was his emerging flair as a romantic cavalier, dazzling young ladies with histrionic flourishes of language about amatory Troys and crossed Rubicons. He and several friends began happily noising themselves about as "the Wreckers," King explaining once with a grin, "We wreck girls." King would usually do the scouting for comely prospects for the rest of them, picking the comeliest for himself.

But in little else did there seem anything particularly remarkable about him during his years at Morehouse, a campus then serving as a kind of gentlemen's finishing academy for the sons of Atlanta's black elect. He proved only a middling student, quiet, self-enclosed, usually lodging himself at the very rear of the classroom. He held vague notions of perhaps escaping his father's ministerial predestination by studying medicine, but with his difficulty with the exactitudes of science, he decided to major in sociology to prepare for a career in law. Beyond that, the only academic intensity he evinced was listening with a transfixed raptness to the weekly addresses of Morehouse president Dr. Benjamin Mays, a nationally prestigious theological scholar. But at the same time, Martin discovered on the Morehouse campus a heady intellectual release from his father's constricting proprieties, with rompingly free discussions about any issue whatsoever, especially the matter of the depredations worked on the black psyche by the South's racist order. And in the course of his sojourn at Morehouse, he happened to encounter for the first time Thoreau's essay *On Civil Disobedience*.

Then, the summer before his last year at Morehouse, in 1947, when he was still only eighteen, he surprisingly elected to enter the ministry after all. It was a curiously heatless decision, "not a miraculous or supernatural something," as he later related, but a conclusion that the church still offered the most promising way to answer "an inner urge to serve humanity" that had begun gathering in him by now. He was already feeling the first vague stirrings of that mysterious impulsion, found in all eventual moral-heroic figures, to give oneself over to some larger truth and purpose and meaning, "to something that transcends our immediate lives," so enlarging one's own life to the historic dimensions of that grander reality. And it was probably inevitable that the central importance of the church in the black community, and consequently the special preeminence of the preacher, would sooner or later invite that impatient ambition of his. He managed to contrive for himself an intellectually suitable peace with the Baptist Church by calculating that he would be a "rational" minister, whose sermons would be "a respectable force for ideas, even social protest."

However studiously qualified his son's decision, though, the senior King was elated. He immediately began arranging for Martin to join him as assistant pastor at Ebenezer, setting the Sunday for him to deliver the requisite "trial sermon" before the congregation. Rising behind the pulpit over which his father had familiarly loomed for years, the junior King, short and stumpy, seemed rather a dwindled edition of the formidable figure his father had always presented. But as he began moving into his sermon to the assembled membership, it was as if he were abruptly, uncannily transfigured from the careless boy who had grown up among them, assuming an almost preternatural magnitude of resonant and assured authority with his polysyllabic unfurlings of language and the passion of his message. . . . As it happened, that message had been lifted from a printed sermon by the notable New York liberal clergyman Harry Emerson Fosdick — an inclination to casual textual appropriation that was to become an unhappy habit of King's — but no one in the congregation could have known that, and when the young King finished, they all swarmed to their feet in a jubilating ovation.

So did King begin his personal exodus out of his past and the old grim Egypt of the black condition in the South — which was ultimately to carry the rest of his people with him, including even his father.

II

Eager to acquire an intellectual freight to match his already voluminous vocabulary, the young King struck out for Crozer Theological Seminary, in Chester, Pennsylvania — a small school of not quite a hundred students, perhaps a quarter of them black, a racial mix still novel in those years, on a campus effervescent with liberal freethinking carbonations. Nevertheless, amid its predominantly white student society, King, always meticulously groomed and elaborately polite, kept himself at first to a somewhat starchy and detached reserve, once reproving another black student for keeping beer in his room because of their responsibility to bear irreproachably "the burdens of the Negro race." This initial stuffiness obliged one black minister, in whose church King served for a while as a student pastor, to apprise Crozer's white faculty that, despite his remarkable pulpit performances, King had "an attitude of aloofness," a certain "snobbishness" and "smugness," that would likely preclude his ever "ministering effectively to the average Negro congregation."

Yet he had turned into a ferociously diligent student, beginning at Crozer a prodigious, systematic campaign — studying in his room often through the night — to compile an intellectual vision for himself, forging through Plato, St. Augustine, Rousseau, Hobbes, Locke, Nietzsche, surveys of Hinduism, Jainism, Islam, as if determined to methodically stalk and capture the final meaning, the Truth, of all life. He became enthralled for a time with Walter Rauschenbusch's "social gospel," which optimistically presumed the improvability of the human condition through a "moral reconstruction of society," replacing "mammonistic capitalism" with a "Christian commonwealth." Duly reading Marx, King was so taken with his titanic indictment of the capitalist system that he contracted what was to be a lifelong antipathy to capitalism's cold and Moloch-like qualities. But he would eventually dismiss Marxism itself as a "grand illusion" of a moral society, "a Christian heresy" with its theology of materialistic determination and moral relativism, which "would argue that the end justifies the means," because "in the long run the end must be preexistent in the means." Becoming further captivated with Thoreau's proposition that "one honest man" could morally regenerate an entire society, King then discovered Gandhi, and the way he transformed Thoreau's principle of individual nonviolent resistance into a seismic popular movement to expunge British power from India, through the enormous "soul force" of a patiently suffering mass resistance, impossibly inconveniencing not only the administrative agencies but the conscience of its rulers. Even so, King did not then trust the relevance of Gandhi's nonviolent resistance to addressing the segregationist system dominating the American South, still suspecting it quite likely that, as he later recalled, "the only way we would solve the problem of segregation was an armed revolt." More realistic seemed to him Reinhold Niebuhr's brinier notion of a perpetual tension between Rauschenbusch's sort of hopeful perspective and the inherent, inveterate sinfulness of self-interest in human nature, most openly expressing itself in "collective evil," in which men in herds will always act more brutishly than as individuals, a propensity extending to nations, governments, corporations, all such large structures of society.

Meanwhile, King had grown assured enough at Crozer to venture from his stolid stiffness and become something of a glad spirit about the campus, to the extent that he was eventually elected president of the student body. He exuberantly took to playing pool, drinking beer himself, pitching into card games, beginning the habit of smoking cigarettes that was to stay with him from then on. He also resumed, from Atlanta, his amorous careering among the young ladies of the environs, several of whom he left, when he graduated, still supposing they were engaged to him.

But during his third year, King fell with abandon into a fevered romance, the most consuming of his life up to that point, with the daughter of an immigrant German woman working as a cook in the school's cafeteria — a girl who happened to be involved with one of his professors when King swooped her away. When his friends realized King had actually arrived at a determination to marry the girl, they vigorously admonished him that an interracial marriage, with the reactions it was sure to provoke from both blacks and whites, would be calamitous to his hopes of ever pastoring a church in the South. Still, King fiercely refused to relinquish the girl, while sinking into a gloom of desperation. Having returned to the student quarters late one night, disheveled from another furtive assignation with her, King roused a friend and blurted in torment, tears welling in his eyes, that while he could brave his father's fury about the marriage, he didn't know how he could face his mother's pain — but still he could not bring himself to lose this girl, lose this love of his life. Nonetheless, after some six months, confronted with the prospect that his passion for her would almost certainly cost him his expanding aspirations for a socially significant Southern ministry, King at last disengaged from the affair — but not without obvious and lingering anguish. It left him "with a broken heart," according to one friend: "He never recovered."

Indeed, it was a loss, caused by the intransigent racial alienations of that time, that lasted like some hole of ever-hungering emptiness throughout his life. But he pushed on to graduate from Crozer as valedictorian, with the highest grade average in his class and a scholarship for further studies.

In the gleaming new green Chevrolet,

complete with "Power Glide," that Daddy King had presented his son for his success at Crozer, King then traveled farther north to Boston, to enter the doctoral program at Boston University. He settled into an apartment across from the Savoy Ballroom, its nightly music whomping through the closed windows of his room as he resumed his voracious studying amid tumbled heaps of books. Even so, he did not confine himself altogether to that room, ranging out regularly to social affairs, a natty young scholarly dandy, to explore what agreeable female company Boston might offer. Rather dispirited by what he came across, he was supplied the phone number of a girl he was assured would not disappoint him.

Coretta Scott, almost two years older than King, was a student at Boston's New England Conservatory of Music, a bright and earnest young woman, a graduate of Antioch College, who was the daughter of a prosperous farmer in Alabama's rural Perry County. She had grown up there a rather solitary and serious girl, with an aspiration before long to levitate from premier singer in the local church choir to a classical concert soloist. Though she was supporting herself during her conservatory studies by working for room and board as a maid in a

Beacon Hill boardinghouse, she yet preserved her poise of a calm and refined gravity, a Creek Indian strain in her mother's ancestry lending her a look of almost Egyptian sculptured sereneness. She would seem to have been virtually a foreordained match for King's own nature.

But when she took his phone call, King startled her by promptly announcing sight unseen, in his pipe organ intonations, "Every Napoleon has his Waterloo, and I'm like Napoleon — I'm at my Waterloo, and I'm on my knees." Coretta was diverted enough to agree at least to have lunch with him. But when he appeared to pick her up the next day, she was disconcerted to find the source of such grandiloquence so squat and prosaic a figure. He transported her in his Power Glide Chevrolet to a cafeteria, where he proceeded to effuse over her looks, then declaimed on everything from Southern-fried soul food to comparative philosophy, until to Coretta, as to the congregation at Ebenezer during his trial sermon, he seemed somehow through the sheer symphonics of his rhetoric to actually grow larger in stature before her eyes. Delivering her back to the conservatory, King finally notified her that "the four things I look for in a wife are character, intelligence, personality, and beauty. You have them all."

Having passed that swiftly from a phone call to a proclamation of intent to take her as his wife, King then conducted a courtship somewhat more measured in pace, consisting mainly of a genteel round of concerts and plays. But they soon found they both felt the same gravitational pull toward some larger cause, like the still submerged but restless urgency of so many other young African Americans over the South at that time, to transform somehow the bleakly repressive world they had grown up in. When Daddy King, though, began to sense his son's unprecedented seriousness about this girl in Boston, he was aghast — he had always meant for him to return to their copastorship in Atlanta and marry a girl of the black establishment there, a number of whom apparently Martin had also proposed to, which the senior King lost no time in imparting to Coretta. In a visit to the King home in Atlanta, then a materialization by Daddy King and his wife in Boston, Coretta was dismayed to note Martin's peculiar deference to his father's bombastic presence, followed by his complaints that she had not sufficiently impressed him.

But at last it was settled. And in the

summer of 1953, before King's final year of study, with Coretta now effectively forsaking her hopes of a career in music, in the front yard of her family's home in Alabama they were married — in a union to seem more a kind of sedate alliance in love not unlike that of, say, a missionary couple. With all hotels and motels anywhere around racially closed to them, they spent their wedding night nearby in the guest bedroom of the residential quarters of a funeral parlor.

Meanwhile, King had been continuing in Boston his assiduous program for accumulating a respectable intellectual capital for his ministry. While he had come to feel uncomfortable with what seemed to him the cheerful naivetés of the standard liberal vision, he yet concluded that Niebuhr was a bit too direly fixated on the incorrigible baseness of human nature. As an accommodation of those two approaches, he took with huge enthusiasm to Hegel's idea of dialecticism: the continuous process in human understanding and history of a prevailing thesis inevitably invoking a contrary antithesis, the two then forming a synthesis that becomes the new thesis to be countered by its antithesis, an interplay endlessly progressing. He also found himself deeply stirred by the school of theological thought called "personalism," with its insistence that the last real measure of meaning in all affairs of the world was how they affected the lot of the individual life, any violation of the worth of the individual being the final definition of evil. In all, King was to arrive in the end at a kind of Christian socialism of conscience, once professing to a friend, "If we are to achieve real equality, the United States will have to adopt a modified form of socialism." Though it was always to remain an essentially Christian perspective that animated him, it could not have been more distant from his father's conventionally conservative Baptist fundamentalism. And in that he had attained his most meaningful personal liberation.

In his long intellectual enterprise, though, King was never to develop into an original thinker himself — his was finally a more didactically interested pursuit, its ends active. For that matter, he was still given, in his course papers and even finally in his doctoral dissertation, to helping himself whole, in whatever careless hurry of impatience, from the works of others without fretting over attribution, a tendency that distressed many, when discoveries of it came decades later, as instances of outright scholastic plagiarism. Despite that, King did prove in time to possess an awesome ability for absorbing and synthesizing the great concepts of other thinkers. And what would emerge as genuinely protean and singular about him was that, after such a laborious assimilation of ideas, he could then, when thrown by happenstance into history in Montgomery, translate those ideas so immediately and spectacularly into immense action. Indeed, few have ever made that crossing from thought to exertion quite so momentously.

And in that crossing, King's might for moving masses would derive finally not from his self-plotted scholarship, but from his initially disdained Pentecostal origins — an almost physical sense, from the soul-shuddering rhetorics of those church services of his boyhood, for the energy and life of language, in which, as one associate observed to biographer Stephen Oates, "the right word, emotionally charged, could reach the whole person and change the relationships of men."

After finishing his last year at Boston University, King resolutely evaded his father's mounting demands that he come back now and share Ebenezer's pulpit with him. Instead, King had found a small but suitably decorous congregation of mostly middle-class, relatively cultivated folk at a church some 170 miles away from Atlanta, in Montgomery, Alabama. Coretta herself was desolated by the decision, having hoped they would begin their life in some more cosmopolitan urban center of the North. But late in August of 1954, after loading their belongings in the green Chevrolet, they headed out of Boston and back down into the wide, mild, hazed, piney countrysides, the dreaming weathers and familiar mellow earths, of their origins, the South.

III

Dexter Avenue Baptist was a small, neat, plain wooden church set just a short distance down the wide boulevard of Dexter Avenue from Alabama's state capitol — a close spacing, the modest black church and white-domed citadel of state power looming atop the hill immediately above it, that was to seem, in the South's racial conflict to come, an improbable bit of symbolic stagecraft. In 1954, the congregation of comparatively affluent, reserved black citizens that gathered in Dexter's sanctuary every Sunday found their young new minister precisely to their respectable tastes — a prodigiously learned young divine, son of a prominent Atlanta preacher, who at twenty-five carried a mandarinlike manner of unfalteringly courtly, somber dignity. In their satisfaction, they had accorded him the highest salary paid any black pastor in the city.

King applied himself to his ministerial responsibilities with a sedulous earnestness. Usually rising before six, he devoted long hours each week to composing and then memorizing his sermon for the next Sunday, finally rehearsing its delivery in front of a full-length bathroom mirror. In his preparation for these messages, he once happily let the membership know, he had read so far a total of 26 books and 102 magazines. The sermons he resonantly delivered to them in their simple little sanctuary each Sunday were perhaps a bit extravagantly laden with allusions to Aquinas, Freud, Carlyle, even Alfred the Great. But they almost unfailingly moved the congregation with their hints, pulsing under the elaborate erudition, of pent compressions of some obscure but immense purpose.

King conscientiously tended to the usual cycle of weddings and funerals, presiding at church socials, reorganizing the church's operating structures, while moving out into wider community involvements, attending sessions of the Alabama Council on Human Relations, joining the Montgomery chapter of the National Association for the Advancement of Colored People (NAACP) — intimating a certain restless stir of larger ambition when he privately allowed that he might run to head it. Through all this, he was still receiving regular letters of energetic instruction and admonition from Daddy King in Atlanta. Meanwhile, he was laboring away as well on his Ph.D. dissertation, a consideration of Tillich's analytical theological calculus against the warmer and more immediate values of personalism — and, whatever its hasty burglaries from the work of others, he was granted his doctorate nine months after arriving in Montgomery. Several months after that, in November of 1955, Coretta gave birth to their first child, a daughter they named Yolanda.

In general, after only a little over a year in Montgomery, King had come to be securely established in a situation of considerable regard in the black community unusual for so young a pastor. Yet all this had taken place within a city of the deep South, the old capital of the Confederacy, whose fifty thousand black citizens still inhabited, among its seventy thousand whites, a separate shadow society of shabbier schools and dingier housing, less than a third with indoor toilet plumbing. Most of Montgomery's blacks were consigned to menial jobs principally supporting the comfort and needs of the white community, only some two thousand of them registered to vote, the lives of them all ruled over by the arbitrary whims and will of a disdainful white power complex.

To fully understand and feel what then followed, one must try to recede somehow in time — back through all the loud winds and flares of the years that have intervened since then, back before Reagan's neoconservative America, on back through the furors and turmoils of Watergate and Vietnam and the storms of the sixties, back before the national trauma of that noon in Dallas — all the way back to what seems now that quiet, static, almost primitively simple and plain age in America's life during the fifties.

On the cold, dim, late Thursday afternoon of December 1, 1955, a forty-two-year-old seamstress named Rosa Parks, a trim, soft-spoken, bespectacled woman of tidily proper comportment, left after a day of working in the tailor shop of a downtown Montgomery department store and, wearily, boarded a city bus home. She took an aisle seat near the middle of the already crowded bus, beside three other black passengers, in the row right behind the front section reserved by law for whites — which rapidly filled until, at the third stop, a white man was left having to stand. The driver turned to demand of Mrs. Parks and the three blacks beside her, "Awright, you folks, I want those seats." The other three black passengers compliantly arose and moved to stand in the back of the bus — but Mrs. Parks did not budge. The driver again demanded she vacate her seat for the white passenger. She then replied, out of a weariness not just from her day's toil but, suddenly, from all the accumulated debasements and indignities of her past years as a black in Montgomery, quietly and simply: "No."

That "No," and Mrs. Parks's arrest, quickly set off the spontaneous combustion among Montgomery's black citizenry of a determination to boycott the city's segregated bus system. Such a confrontation, actually, had already been building. The year before, the Supreme Court's *Brown* decision, unanimously declaring school segregation unconstitutional, had sent a wind of exhilaration through the black community, quickening a restive impatience with the entire architecture of segregation. More particularly, several prior incidents of black women forced from their seats to make room for whites had produced a mounting mood for some sort of protest action. Mrs. Parks herself, for that matter, had not simply bloomed forth out of a political void: she had long served, to the discomfort of her husband, a barber, as a conscientious member and sometimes officer of the local NAACP chapter, an organization then regarded by most white Southerners as a subversive mischief-monger; had even passed a week at the interracial social rights training retreat in the North Carolina mountains called the Highlander Folk School; and had assisted in several voter registration programs among Montgomery's blacks. With her arrest now for refusing to surrender her bus seat to a white, Montgomery's veteran black rights activist at that time, a bulky-fisted Pullman porter named E. D. Nixon, enthused, "This is the case!" Almost immediately, mimeographed leaflets calling for a boycott of the city's bus line that following Monday were coursing through the city's black neighborhoods.

But when, the night of Mrs. Parks's arrest, Nixon phoned the young pastor of Dexter Avenue Baptist to ask him to join in the boycott movement, King, out of some uneasiness beyond just his absorption in his multiple other duties, seemed curiously reluctant: "Brother Nixon, let me think on it awhile, and call me back." Concerned at King's hesitation, Nixon called Ralph Abernathy, the twenty-nine-year-old minister of Montgomery's oldest black Baptist church, who had already become King's closest friend — a stocky, slow badger of a man with a drowsy-eyed, drooping face but a droll and rollicking earthiness, who in their special comradeship over the years was to serve as something like King's Falstaff. Abernathy then called King to exhort him about the elemental importance of cooperating in this boycott effort. King finally agreed to lend it his support if it would not entail his having to aid in any of the organizing, and he consented at least to an initial leadership meeting being held at Dexter the next afternoon, a Friday. After that meeting, though, King wound up mimeographing with Abernathy in the church basement a revised copy of the leaflet announcing the Monday boycott. And the next evening, he made a tour with Abernathy of the town's black nightspots to promote the boycott and urge an orderly calm.

Arising before dawn on Monday morning, King hastened with a cup of coffee to the front window of his house and saw, to his amazed elation, three buses that were normally filled with black riders now roll past in the dark with their lit interiors all spookily empty. He plunged out to his car and, driving alone around the early morning streets for about an hour, beheld other buses carrying only scant smatterings of whites — and, in the morning's emerging cold gray light, hundreds of blacks trudging along the sidewalks to their jobs, others riding piled in the cars of friends and relatives.

Still somewhat dazed at this massive initial success, King and Montgomery's black leadership collected again that afternoon, before the mass rally that night in one of the larger black churches, for the business of forming an overall organization, named at Abernathy's suggestion the Montgomery Improvement Association (MIA), to direct the boycott campaign. The question then arose of who was to be put forward as the leader of this whole affair. With a surprising swiftness, though at twenty-six he still struck some as "more like a boy than a man" — and mostly because he was a relatively fresh figure not yet entangled in the politics of ego within the city's black establishment — King found himself the only person nominated. Stunned, when asked if he would accept the position King responded with the minimal assent, "If you think I can render some service, I will."

Right after that, as King was back home preparing for the mass meeting that night, where he was to present the major address in his sudden new role as leader of the boycott movement, he was overcome with a kind of dread, "possessed by fear," he later confessed, and "obsessed by a feeling of inadequacy." At dusk he set out, without supper, to the meeting site, he and Abernathy driven there by an old Morehead friend of King's. They found the church surrounded for blocks around by some four thousand of Montgomery's black populace. As they left the car and began making their way toward the church, the crowd, teeming around them in the warm December evening, parted to let them pass with a spreading rustle of clapping, which rapidly swelled to a vast surf of applause. King murmured to the driver in a momentary abstraction of wonder, "You know, Finley, this could turn into something big."

Reaching the church, where loudspeakers had been set up for the enormous crowd dammed outside, King and Abernathy entered to a detonation of cheers and clapping from the thousand people packed into the sanctuary. After they were all led in a huge swinging of voices through the old revival hymn —

What a fellowship, what a joy divine,
Leaning on the everlasting arms!
What a blessedness, what a peace is mine,
Leaning on the everlasting arms! . . .

— King took the pulpit. As the moment has been masterfully recounted by Taylor Branch in the first volume of his chronicle of the civil rights movement, King looked over this assembly massed before him, many of whom he still didn't know, and finally began, "We are here this evening" — pausing then for just an instant — "for serious business." Over an answering murmuration from his audience, King's voice rolled on now with the even and majestic deliberation of a gathering inevitability:

We are here in a general sense, because

first and foremost — we are American citizens. And we are determined to apply our citizenship, to the fullness of its means. . . . But we are here in a specific sense, because of the bus situation in Montgomery.

To a rising anticipatory rumbling at each of his lines, King invoked the history behind the incident of three evenings ago, explained how they must all at last reply with a collective community protest to this arrest of Rosa Parks, "not one of the finest Negro citizens, but one of the finest citizens in Montgomery." He again hung for a moment.

You know, my friends, there comes a *time,* when people get tired of being trampled over by the iron feet of oppression —

Abruptly there exploded an astonishing thunderclap of cheering, shouts, and stomping feet, seeming briefly to startle King as it stormed on to an accompanying roar a second later from the greater throng gathered outside — it had become, in fact, the birth of all the mass meetings to come in black churches and tabernacles over the

South in the years ahead. King's voice tolled on over the tumult:

There comes a time, my friends, when people get *tired* of being thrown across the abyss of humiliation, where they experience the bleakness of nagging despair. There comes a time when people get tired of being pushed out of the glittering sunlight of life's July and left standing amidst the piercing chill of an Alpine November. There —

His voice was again lost in the ovation loosed by these phrases, no matter how improbably baroque in formulation. What would always prove the genius, the peculiar eloquence, of King's otherwise cumbersomely ornate metaphors was that they were the rhetoric of the human spirit immensely and elaborately gathering itself for slow and terrific struggle. He pealed on:

Now, let us say that we are not here advocating violence, we have overcome that. I want it to be known throughout Montgomery and throughout this nation that we are — a *Christian* people. . . . But the great glory of American democracy is the right to protest for right. . . . And if we are wrong, the Supreme Court of this nation is wrong. If we are wrong, God Almighty is wrong! . . .

King's shouts were now riding on the mounting tide of cries, clapping, trampling feet, seconded by the roar from the vast throng in the dark outside — he released at last into that passion and power the Dexter congregation had always sensed under his Sunday morning sermons, in a soul communion now beyond all scholarship and politics and legalisms:

> . . . If we are wrong, Jesus of Nazareth was merely a utopian dreamer and never came down to earth! If we are wrong, justice is a lie. . . . And we are determined here in Montgomery to work and fight, until justice runs down like water and righteousness as a mighty stream!

It was the most dramatic instance yet of King's sharing that mystic capability of leaders of genius, at certain critical moments, to suddenly transmute into someone, something, awesomely larger than their ordinary selves. In an ovation that kept thundering on and on, he then began making his way back up the aisle of the church, with people leaning and reaching to touch him as he passed.

It had begun.

The actual demands of Montgomery's bus boycott campaign would seem, from this distance of history, almost abjectly modest: merely a free-shifting arrangement in which blacks would seat themselves from the rear forward, whites from the front toward the rear, with neither required to surrender their seat once settled in it. Drivers would accord all passengers equal courtesy. And blacks, who constituted about three-fourths of all bus patrons, would at least be allowed to make application, for serious consideration, to become drivers on primarily black routes. King himself, in rather boggling contrast to his mass meeting forensics, even assured local reporters and city authorities that "we are not asking for an end to segregation" — though he did confide to one reporter that he personally regarded all segregation as a colossal sin. But so timorous an appeal did it seem that it prompted spirited complaints from the NAACP and its executive secretary, Roy Wilkins, always wary about popular protest initiatives breaking out beyond the NAACP's own carefully calibrated program of courtroom challenges — Wilkins's special prickliness about King to persist, actually, up to King's death.

With such a relatively unpresumptuous petition, though, the black community entertained the most buoyant expectations that, as Abernathy later related, "this would all be over within three or four days." Despite stray gutterings of violence — shots fired at buses emptied by the boycott — King himself assumed the whole matter would be settled in only a few weeks at the most. But he shortly realized he was caught in something far longer and larger than that.

In many ways, this beginning struggle in Montgomery was to contain the genetic code, as it were, of almost all to follow in King's future. In initial negotiating sessions, the boycott's leaders met with instant and intractable resistance from the city, alternating between neighborly amiableness and tight-jawed, gimlet-eyed, choleric outrage. To one bus line spokesman, it could mean that blacks "would go about boasting of a victory they had won over white people." A suspicion quickly set in among many whites that the whole troublesome business had to be the handiwork of sinister forces outside the South, liberal New York agitators and no doubt Communists, because, as one white citizen put it, in their hometown of Montgomery "the niggers are not that smart." Montgomery's mayor decreed, "The white people are firm in their convictions that they do not care whether the Negroes ever ride a city bus again if it means that the social fabric of our community is to be destroyed."

Confronted by such a mentality, MIA's leadership soon realized that negotiations would avail nothing for the time being. Meanwhile, to compensate for the loss of bus transportation on which the black community so hugely depended, the MIA enlisted Montgomery's black taxi fleet to provide rides for only a minimal fare — which the city swiftly countered by threatening the arrest of any driver not charging the statutory higher rate. With that, the movement leadership mobilized the massive, intricately coordinated car-pool operation that was to carry the boycott on through the subsequent grueling months, with more than two hundred volunteer drivers supplying some twenty thousand rides a day — a communal feat not a little evocative of the civilian boat lift at Dunkirk, only in this case maintained week after week. To this the city responded with a running siege of random police pounces, scattering groups waiting at pickup sites, stopping car-pool drivers to check headlights and windshield wipers, issuing citations for whimsical traffic violations.

The city's consternation had, of course, rapidly come to focus on King in particular. White officials began styling him as an upstart provocateur posing the main impediment to any resolution of this unfortunate discord in the long amity between Montgomery's white and black citizens. Word was additionally distributed about that he was helping himself to MIA funds, a claim arising out of the same cynicism of some sure self-interest, an incapacity to otherwise comprehend what truly animated him, that was to constitute — not only from Montgomery's white burghers but soon from presidents and many journalists as well as J. Edgar Hoover — one of King's most harrying tribulations in the years ahead.

But as the confrontation in Montgomery wore on far beyond King's original suppositions, it was as if he sensed himself being gradually enfolded into some wider embrace of fate. He declared, "We are caught in a great moment of history — it is bigger than Montgomery." And like an untried actor suddenly finding himself cast in a far greater play than he'd ever reckoned on, he began flexing his potential, testing his arts over the course of his messages through the following months, his full vision emerging only through that long succession of mass meeting exhortations.

Those exhortations had already begun prompting speculations among some that he could just turn out the American Gandhi, but he still had only a summary familiarity with Gandhi's ideas and meaning. While rapidly applying himself to learning more about this figure increasingly cited now as his possible antecedent, he yet averred later, "This business of passive resistance and nonviolence is the gospel of Jesus. I went to Gandhi through Jesus."

Indeed, King was to operate always from the surpassingly religious, if not mystical, gospel he came to preach night after night at those rallies in churches around Montgomery. In every human being, black or white, there exists, however dimly, a certain natural identification with every other human being, so that we tend to feel that what happens to a fellow human being also in some way happens to us. Therefore no man can very long continue to abuse another human being without beginning to feel in himself at least some dull answering stir of discomfort. And in the catharsis of a live confrontation with wrong, when an oppressor's violence is met with a forgiving love, he can be vitally touched and even, however partially or momentarily, reborn as a human being — "You are shaming them into decency," King announced to his congregations — while the society witnessing such a confrontation will be quickened in conscience toward compassion and justice. "The end is reconciliation, the end is redemption, the end is the creation of the Beloved Community," he declared, and called out to Montgomery's white officials from the pulpits of its black churches, "We will meet your physical force with soul force. We will not hate you, but we will not obey your evil laws. We will soon wear you down by our capacity to suffer."

From the beginning, some were suggesting it was a proposition that simply presumed too much of the species. And in later years, King himself would arrive at certain equivocations on its grand terms, offering once, "A law may not make a man love me, but it can stop him from lynching me." Still, he never ceased to believe, as he preached those nights in Montgomery, that "nonviolence can touch men where the law cannot reach them," by appealing to those "who have allowed their consciences to sleep," with the result that "the most prejudiced mind in Montgomery, in America, can become a loving mind, a mind of goodwill." When he was eventually arrested, he proclaimed that even "if we are trampled every day, don't ever let anyone pull you down so low as to hate them. We must use the weapon of love, we must have compassion and understanding for those who hate us." It was all, he explained once, the Greek concept of agape, that highest, transcendent love for all humankind, and what was happening in Montgomery he finally cast on a cosmic scale: "The fight here is between light and darkness." A favorite line of his began to emerge: "The arc of the moral universe is long, and it bends toward justice."

Only gradually in these pentecostalisms did King begin to mention Gandhi's nonviolent struggle in India as a precedent for challenging the South's segregationist order. In fact, the harder practical reality was that even with his gospel of agape, King would face considerably more forbidding odds than those that confronted Gandhi, who had the overwhelming force of the Indian multitudes who could easily arrest, through their sheer preponderant numbers, the workings of the Raj. But for King, with African Americans a minority, the popular weight was tilted heavily against him. Beyond that, King was hardly contending with an alien colonial presence, but with the laws and passions of the local native majority, for whom the stakes — the unknown dislocations, the forebodings — were much more intimate and immediate. In this, King had nothing finally to rely on or appeal to but the notice and conscience of the rest of the nation — the press, the powers in Washington, the democratic principles of the law of the Republic. And the only way to reach that national constituency beyond the South was for the Southern black to engage in a moral theater of direct public confrontation with the whole apparatus of segregation, so precipitating those cathartic clashes — violent moments of truth — in which the white segregationist was compelled "to commit his brutality openly, in the light of day, with the rest of the world looking on."

This dynamic of "surfacing tensions," as he termed it, necessarily depended on the larger public witness of the national news media, and it wasn't long before the conflict in Montgomery began to fetch their attention — this embryonic, obscure inception of the historical saga to come first glimpsed by the nation in the ashen gray-and-black news footage of that day. King himself quickly caught the special fascination of the press — a twenty-six-year-old Baptist preacher who, with his evangelisms about loving one's oppressors into redemption, had apparently become the novel Moses of the boycott movement. He struck many as implausibly young for so heavy a role, and also, it did not escape their notice, as having taken on a matching heaviness of manner, a certain pontifical propoundment in discourse and a bearing of bishoplike somberness. But Montgomery was the beginning of a symbiosis with the press, and especially with the coinciding genesis of its TV age, that was to become critical to the movement's progress from then on — just as there had begun forming a new electronic kind of public nervous system of consciousness and conscience through television's mass direct observance. So mortal to the movement did King already sense this new factor to be that, in later years when demonstrations were lagging, he would impatiently urge his aides, "We've got to get something going. The press is leaving. . . . It was a mistake not to march today. In a crisis, we must have a sense of drama."

With the magnifying notice of the press, the MIA suddenly found itself with a tide of funds spilling into Montgomery from such diverse sources as the United Auto Workers, sympathizers around the globe from Paris to New Delhi, with even the stodgier NAACP, despite its antipathy to street protests, stirred to contribute. There had also arrived by now in Montgomery — but somewhat discreetly, so as not to excite the already malarial fantasies of whites there, and much to the unease of the MIA's leadership itself — a freelance, uncontainably eager, veteran social activist from Greenwich Village named Bayard Rustin, a long, willowy figure, exquisitely cultivated, with a patrician brandy-brown face and debonair West Indian accent. However exotic an article, Rustin, out of his long experience as a pacifist and partisan and organizer with A. J. Muste and civil rights elder statesman A. Philip Randolph, was to serve as a vital adviser to King in his beginning years. But he also happened to carry what was regarded at that time as a rather gamey past, a member of the Young Communist League in the thirties and a homosexual once jailed in California on a morals charge — this worrisome baggage eventually compelling him to withdraw from an official working association with King, not without some bitterness at the alacrity with which King agreed to accept his resignation.

Nevertheless, Rustin had come to Montgomery recognizing that what was developing there, as he enthused in a working paper for the MIA, "challenges the entire social, political, and economic order that has kept us second-class citizens," and "those who oppose us understand this."

In this excitement, Rustin was among a growing number of others descended from America's old radical-progressive past — that militantly egalitarian, socialist dream once of the Wobblies, Joe Hill, Big Bill Haywood, that was revived in the strifes of the thirties — successors to that long revolutionary under-history of America who thought they now spied in Montgomery the possible dawning into reality at last of their millennial hopes. Rustin was to work in informal concert, as private advisers to King, with another seasoned social rights crusader from that long-balked but enduring tradition — Stanley Levison, a wealthy New York attorney who had made his fortune not in law, but from real estate and car dealerships. A plain, pale man in bulky dark-frame glasses, with something of a bureaucrat's baggy drabness of look, Levison, while never forsaking a scrupulous devotion to privacy, had remained since his student days during the Depression a dedicated social militant, involved in early civil rights initiatives in the South as well as organizing financial support for the Communist Party during the McCarthy years — though he was later to stoutly deny ever having been a member of the Party himself. His political history, in any event, hardly dismayed King, and Levison was to become his closest and most trusted white friend, King relying on him not only as a strategic counselor, but as editor and effectively ghostwriter of his subsequent books, adviser on drafting speeches, even for preparing his tax returns. Levison, on his part, as related by Taylor Branch, startled his wife after meeting King personally for the first time by effusing that he was "his only true friend in the world." There seemed, in all, some curious, instant, profound, total rapport between them, more than simply a mutual enthusiasm between common believers. But it was also to turn out, for King, an alliance producing nightmarish consequences.

At times King still seemed stunned by how the boycott movement had begun ramifying, an old friend from his Crozer days finding that "he wanders around in a daze asking himself, *Why has God seen fit to catapult me into such a situation?*" Then one afternoon, after he had picked up three black citizens to drop them off at a car-pool pickup point, there took place the first of his many arrests to come. Two motorcycle policemen pulled him over for purportedly ignoring a 25-mph speed limit zone. Ordered out of his car, he was frisked, promptly bundled into the back of a squad car, and transported to the northern fringes of Montgomery, silent, trembling, his mind suddenly gone empty, to be clapped into the city's murky and reeking jail. A cold certainty seized him, he later confided, that he would shortly be spirited out of the jail and lynched. The trauma of that first arrest was to leave him forever afterward, no matter how many more times he would be imprisoned, with a dread of finding himself abruptly snatched out of his own world into the hands of a malevolent white authority, kept captive and helpless in a nether region of menace, isolated with only his own glooms and self-doubts.

As word of his arrest rippled rapidly through the black community, a throng began collecting outside the jail, until the chief jailer deemed it prudent to release King on his own recognizance. That night, there unfolded in black churches across Montgomery a serial jubilee of some seven mass meetings. But King, now under a barrage of venomous phone calls and reports of plots to kill him, was "faltering," he later confessed, "and growing in fear." He even briefly acquired a pistol, until Rustin, on a visit to King's home, glimpsed it lying in a chair and reproved King about the bizarreness of an apostle of nonviolence arming himself with a gun. The second evening after his jailing, returning home late from an MIA planning session, with Coretta asleep, he picked up the ringing phone to hear: "Listen, nigger, we tired of you and your mess. If you aren't out of this town in three days, we gonna blow your brains out and blow up your house." After slapping the phone down, he went into the kitchen to make some coffee, all prospects of sleep gone. And as he sat with his cup at the kitchen table, he was overwhelmed with woe over his own unworthiness, his life of bourgeois privilege even during this ordeal into which he had led the city's black commonry, and finally about the superficiality of his "inherited" call into the ministry, although he "had never felt an experience with God in the way that you must . . . if you're going to walk the lonely paths of this life." As he later recalled that late night hour of desolation, "I couldn't take it any longer" and "tried to think of a way to move out of the picture without appearing a coward." Dropping his head into his hands, he suddenly realized he was praying aloud in the midnight hush of the kitchen: "Lord, I'm down here trying to do what's right. . . . But Lord, I'm faltering, I'm losing my courage. And I can't let the people see me like this. . . . But I've come to the point where I can't face it alone." And at that moment, as King would tell it, he seemed to hear "an inner voice . . . the voice of Jesus," answering him: "Martin Luther, stand up for righteousness, stand up for justice, stand up for truth. And lo, I will be with you, even until the end of the world." That voice of Jesus, King recounted, "promised never to leave me, no, never to leave me alone."

And with that, King would report, all his despairs vanished. It may well have been from that midnight kitchen epiphany, in fact, that King would maintain through all the turmoils of the years afterward his peculiar mien of an almost galactic remoteness, as if the deepest center of him were lost in a secret communion with something far beyond the furors of the moment. At the least, it was an exaltation that had come to him that evening with fortunate timing to brace him for what was to follow four nights later.

As King was conducting a mass meeting at Abernathy's church, a bomb exploded on the front porch of his home, wrecking the front parlor. King rushed back to find Coretta and their infant daughter safe in a back room, but the yard and street were filled with an angry churn of some three hundred blacks, many with guns and knives, in a pandemonium of reporters, white policemen skirmishing to keep some order in the bedlam of howled threats, all in a wailing of sirens. It was the first time that King faced the crisis, to close in on him during his last years, of the nonviolent integrity he had imparted to the movement disintegrating into riot and vengeance. Standing in the shattered glass and rubble of his front porch, he lifted a hand to still the uproar and cried out, "We are not advocating violence! We want to love our enemies — be *good* to them. This is what we must live by, we must meet hate with love. We must love our white brothers no matter what they do to us. Love them, and let them know you love them. . . ." (One white policeman afterward acknowledged that he likely owed his life that night to "that nigger preacher.") Even so, King went on, "if I am stopped, this movement will not be stopped. . . . For what we are doing is right, what we are doing is just, and God is with us!"

King and his family were taken to the home of a member of his Dexter congregation to stay the rest of the night — and there, around four in the morning, with a furious battering on the front door, Daddy King appeared. Having driven straight over from Atlanta, he immediately boomed that the time had manifestly come for King to withdraw from Montgomery and return with him to Atlanta, that this boycott business had obviously broken out into something unmanageably wild and dangerous. King hotly answered that he could not abandon this effort now with the great moral stakes that had come to be invested in it — to which Daddy King blared, in despair, "Better to be a live dog than a dead lion!" The two of them argued on until dawn. But King still refused to be taken into this reach for him now by his father. More than one battle, as it had developed, was under way for King in Montgomery.

But the boycott movement remained locked in a dead impasse with intransigent city authorities, a mere static contest, as the MIA disconsolately recognized, of "which side could hold out the longer" and "wear the other side down." Meanwhile, the legions of Montgomery's ordinary black citizens, without bus transport, pressed on through the wet blusters and hot blaze of the changing seasons, laboring to get back and forth from their jobs, to manage their shopping, to somehow keep their lives going.

At last, the boycott's leadership resorted to the course to which the NAACP had long been exclusively devoted and now readily lent its impressive resources to facilitate — a frontal suit in federal court. But when, in June, a three-judge panel ruled the city's system of bus segregation unconstitutional, the city instantly announced it would simply appeal the decision, boding thereby a legal process of possibly years during which the enormous effort of the boycott, the car pool, and the mass meetings would somehow have to be carried on. More unsettling, the city had retaliated to the MIA's federal suit by arranging for a local grand jury to issue mass indictments of some 115 of the MIA's leadership, King to be the first tried, for violating the state's antiboycott laws. The expenses to the MIA of defending against these indictments promised to be staggering, perilously depleting funds for sustaining the boycott through coming months.

Then, with the boycott having hauled on now for astonishingly close to a year, the city delivered its final, potentially devastating blow — asking, before a state court sure to grant it, for an injunction against the car-pool operation as an unlicensed system of municipal transportation. Caught in the likely fatal stranglehold of this latest threat — it was almost literally at the last moment, as King was sitting in the courtroom where the city's petition was being presented to an obviously agreeably disposed judge — the news suddenly came that the Supreme Court had just summarily upheld that bus segregation in Montgomery was indeed unconstitutional. And in that way, not with high theater, but a quiet judicial word, did the year-long boycott movement end at last in triumph.

Whatever King's relief and exultation, he seemed oddly muted afterward, merely remarking mildly to reporters that it was time to "move from protest to reconciliation." And in truth, it had not finally been the boycott campaign of subsequent legend that had defeated the city's unbudging resistance to ending its bus segregation, but the corollary suit in the federal courts. That legal challenge may have been dramatized by the mass protests, but without the suit intervening and prevailing in the end, the Montgomery bus boycott movement, with its mass meetings, King's grand oratorical fugues, its intrepid car-pool operation, all could well have come to a dismal confoundment.

Nevertheless, a year since the quiet "No" uttered by Rosa Parks on that cold afternoon, it was all over. And twelve months after he had peered through his kitchen window into the early morning dark to discover that the bus boycott had marvelously taken, when the first bus now pulled up at the corner near his house under this new order of law, King himself was the first to board it, he and a friend taking with a sober ceremoniousness a seat near the front.

Not unpredictably, glares of violence followed the movement's court victory. Two nights later, a shotgun blast blew in the front door of King's home. Several buses came under rifle fire. Then an early morning bomb explosion reduced to shambles the home of the Lutheran minister of a black church who had been one of the few local whites openly supporting the campaign, and another bomb shortly went off at Abernathy's home, followed by four more explosions at black churches, including Abernathy's. This barrage of violence served to sink King into a deep undertow of guilt. In an address to a mass meeting that strangely prefigured the one he would deliver in Memphis on the last night of his life, he shocked the congregation by suddenly blurting out, "Lord, I hope no one will have to die as a result of our struggle for freedom here in Montgomery. Certainly I don't want to die. But if anyone has to die, let it be me!" And he strangled into tears, so stricken that he clutched the sides of the pulpit, unable to utter anything further, until two ministers on the podium arose and led him back to his chair.

This early had he come to dwell in a constant anticipation of death, aware of the impossible outrage he provoked in many whites and feeling himself enacting the same scenario of crucifixion he would invoke that last night some twelve years later in Memphis. He told his Dexter congregation one Sunday morning, after twelve sticks of dynamite with a burnt-out fuse had been found the night before on his front porch, "I'm not afraid of anybody this morning. . . . If I had to die tomorrow morning, I would die happy. Because I've been to the mountaintop and I've *seen* the Promised Land." His later aide, Andrew

Young, would remember, "He thought in everything he did, it meant his death." About the only answer he provided himself to that abiding fatal expectation was, as he would muse to one gathering, "all of eternity stands with you, and the angels stand beside you, and you know you are right." Yet he could not resist periodic cold washes of terror, seeming at such moments to withdraw into an unreachable melancholy. After a bomb threat on the eve of the Selma campaign, he brooded to his companions, "I've told you all that I don't expect to survive this revolution," and to demurrals that he was simply being morbid, he insisted, "I'm just being realistic." During an early march in Selma, he motioned a colleague over to murmur, "Come on, walk with me, Joe. This may be my last walk."

King would in fact, aside from the constant shadow of bomb and assassination threats, be personally attacked a number of times over the years. At an appearance at a Harlem department store to promote his first book, he was stabbed in the chest with a letter opener by a demented middle-aged black woman, a strike so close to his aorta that he was told afterward he would have died if he had sneezed: the surgery to remove the weapon left a little cross-shaped scar over his heart. Then on a plane flight, a white passenger fell on him with milling fists; and again, as he was registering at a formerly segregated hotel in Selma, a racist youth walloped him on his temple, dropping King to the floor, where the youth kicked him savagely before onlookers intervened. But in each of these physical assaults, King's manner would be much like that peculiarly calm, detached resignation with which as a boy he had received his father's whippings. In Birmingham, as he was addressing a Southern Christian Leadership Conference gathering, another white youth, a member of the American Nazi Party, leapt onto the stage and slugged him on his right cheek; but King made no move, simply accepting several more blows from the youth, gazing at him with his arms dropped to his sides, until aides finally wrestled the assailant away from him. Even then King told them, "Don't hurt him, we have to pray for him."

In the widening beleaguerment of his latter years, it would sometimes seem as if he were, as in the Keats ode, "half in love with easeful death," almost wishful for its surcease from all travail, proposing once that he just might withdraw into a fast "unto death." A Hollywood producer, discussing with King the possibility of a film about his life, idly asked him how he thought it might end, and King responded, "It ends with me getting killed."

King found himself after Montgomery swept up into a dizzying national renown. Though the struggle he led had only been won finally by the federal court suit, yet it had translated King, in that stark segregationist era, into the symbolic figure of a potential civil rights revolution among the South's blacks. He became the focus of a *New York Times Magazine* account of the Montgomery movement, was brought onto *Meet the Press*, would soon appear on the cover of *Time*. He had begun appearing at civic rallies and church convocations far beyond Montgomery, meeting with fanfares of enthusiasm immeasurably vaster than anything he had ever experienced in the South. Received along with other black notables of that time by President Eisenhower in the Oval Office, he was invited before long to Ghana for its celebration of independence from Britain's colonial custodianship, then to India for a monthlong tour of the sites of Gandhi's nonviolent mass struggle, visiting with his surviving disciples. This swiftly had he passed from pastor of a small black church in downtown Montgomery to a figure of international dimension.

But this supernova of fame cast him into a certain dislocation, "caused him some real pain," remembered an MIA official, "in terms of what his life was all about and where he was going." He would even admit to concerns about "reaching the zenith of my career too early," that "I might be on the decline at a fairly early age." At the same time, he was filled with trepidations of inadequacy, the sense of a strange unreality in which it seemed it was someone wholly other and beyond himself who was being celebrated. In a television interview in London, he confessed that "it is never easy for me to accept the role of symbol, without going through constant moments of self-examination." He became, if anything, even more stiffly reserved in manner, "quiet and very, very shy," as Stanley Levison was to remember, with "a certain arm's-length approach." Even to close aides he seemed "very lonely," as one would recall, "despite the fact he was surrounded by people all the time." Though hardly averse to lifting a glass or two with friends, he kept that predilection, along with his cigarette smoking, carefully out of the public eye. He seemed, in all, curiously displaced and stranded in the windy expanses of his new elevation. He pleaded to Harry Belafonte, who was to become a lifelong confidant, "I need your help. I have no idea where this movement is going."

Nevertheless, "I can't stop now," he declared to his Dexter congregation. "History has thrust something upon me from which I cannot turn away." During the boycott, actually, his perspectives on what was under way in Montgomery had already begun widening to the surprising reach of his pronouncing it "part of a worldwide movement. The vast majority of the people of the world are colored. Today many are free. We are part of that great movement. We want no classes or castes. We want to see everybody free." Now he proposed to "expand the struggle on all fronts" and this early began decrying "the madness of militarism" and "an economic system which takes necessities from the masses to give luxuries to the classes." He ventured that "the Negro cannot be free as long as there are poor and underprivileged white people. Equality for Negroes is related to the greater problem of economic uplift for Negroes and poor white men." It was still almost a decade before he would mount his final, cycloramically ambitious Poor People's Campaign, but already he had contracted an obsession "to save the soul of America," as he professed. To his congregation at Dexter, he declaimed, from the words of Isaiah, that "somehow every valley shall be exalted, every hill shall be made low, the crooked places shall be made straight and the rough places plain. The glory of the Lord shall be revealed, and all flesh shall see it together. . . . They shall see it from Montgomery! They shall see it from New York! They shall see it from Ghana, they shall see it from China! For I can look out and see a great number, as John saw, marching into the great eternity, because God is working in this world!" And again preaching his last speech in Memphis, he intoned, "Then we will be in Canaan's freedom-land! Moses might not get to see Canaan, but his children will see it. . . ."

King already suspected that blacks' gaining the vote would be "the key to the whole solution of the South's problem." And to expand the Montgomery movement with desegregation and voter registration campaigns across the rest of the South, he set about fashioning, to the considerable irritation of Roy Wilkins and the NAACP, an organization of his own, chiefly comprising black churchmen from across the South, which would eventually be named the

Southern Christian Leadership Conference (SCLC). Not insignificantly, it was to be headquartered not in Montgomery, but in Atlanta, on Auburn Avenue, the "Sweet Auburn" of King's boyhood. And in November of 1959, after three years at Dexter Avenue Baptist, King decided to move to Atlanta himself and at last accept a co-pastorship with his father at Ebenezer. Having by now forged spectacularly beyond his father, he could finally return as, incontestably, his own man. Daddy King undertook to assure everyone that "he's not coming to cause trouble," announcing with swells of gratification that can only be imagined, "Instead of that, he's chosen the pulpit."

Indeed, King's own civil rights assertions in Atlanta, whether in deference to his father's position there or his own lingering hometown sentiments, were to prove rather glancing and halfhearted over the years. When, in 1960, student sit-ins at segregated restaurants were chain-combusting over the South, young black activists in Atlanta implored King to lend his stature to a series of turbulent sit-ins there, but he seemed oddly, painfully hesitant. Then one evening, at a mass meeting to consider a settlement for the desegregation of the city's stores and restaurants, Daddy King, who had come to be caught up himself now in the popular phenomenon loosed by his son, arose to defend before the student activists there the arrangement reached with Atlanta's civic establishment — only to be met with a blizzard of jeering. King had slipped in late for the meeting, and from the back of the church he watched his father bluster on unavailingly about his own lifetime's long experience as a proud black man out of south Georgia grappling with Atlanta's segregationist society; but his usually commanding thunders were helpless against this barrage of laughter and derision. Finally King pushed his way down the crowded aisle and mounted the rostrum, his unexpected appearance subduing the outcry against his father. As he took the pulpit, tears were in his eyes. "I'm surprised at you," he began, and in a low, even voice, heavy with hurt and indignation, he proceeded to array his high vision of the movement now rising across the South, how it required both the long perspective of elders like his father and the impatient militancy of the younger generation here in this church. He then deplored the "cancer of disunity" in judging this "first written contract" ever committed to by Atlanta's white leadership for the desegregation of its public life, and finished: "If this contract is broken, it will be a disaster and disgrace. If anyone breaks this contract, let it be the white man." With that, almost solely on the power of King's impromptu appeal, the settlement was accepted — and thus, his father vindicated.

He had, then, some twelve years after fleeing Atlanta and his father's dominion, returned to step forth this evening to rescue his father from the tumults of the new day that he had largely inspired. He had wound up now his father's protector.

The Wilderness Time

Even before transferring to his new base in Atlanta, King had begun wheeling out over the country in a perpetual odyssey of personal appearances and addresses, winging from New York to Los Angeles to New Orleans for fund-raising rallies, celebrity benefit concerts with the likes of Sammy Davis, Jr., Frank Sinatra, and Tony Bennett, as if on some sort of interminable campaign tour, passing through so many airport lobbies that he soon averred he could recognize each one simply by its smell. This incessant traveling — which was to largely occupy the rest of his life — was mostly to muster support and financing for a South-wide expansion of "the Montgomery experience," as it had come to be almost religiously referred to. He had confessed to a friend after Montgomery, "I'm worried to death that people will be expecting me to pull rabbits out of a hat for the rest of my life." Yet he seemed obsessed with performing something much like that, endlessly pitching about for some new front of engagement in swings through the Mississippi Delta, South Carolina, Georgia, Virginia, sometimes delivering more than a dozen speeches in three days, billowing out his moral metaphors, "For too long have we been trampled under the iron feet of oppression, *too long* bound in the starless midnight of racism. . . ."

But King was discovering, without the dramatic compressions of an immediate crisis like the Montgomery boycott, the limits of soul rhetoric. Despite the delirious receptions greeting him everywhere, it produced no new popular upsurges of struggle, did nothing finally to begin loosening the total hold of segregation on the South. He found himself hung, as it were, in a kind of oratorical limbo. But, while betraying signs of a growing dislocation and dismay, he kept himself ceaselessly on the move, from locale to locale, from speech to speech, as if sheer headlong motion and peroration had somehow become meaning, action, in themselves.

In fact, King had passed into what would be a prolonged season now of fitful and indefinite drift, his compass still unfixed, in a continuous shifting of tentative and inconclusive initiatives. He entertained the whimsy for a time of styling his operation after Billy Graham's "crusade" system of gigantically mobilized revival extravaganzas in carefully selected and precultivated communities, even consulting privately with Graham and delivering a prayer at one of his amphitheater services. He also made a try at attaching as an instrument for his movement the prodigious logistical resources of the National Baptist Convention, the nation's largest black religious body, but was promptly swatted back by its fearsomely territorial president. Almost as perfervidly as segregationist authorities, actually, the nation's black power estate in general, from its religious grandees to Adam Clayton Powell to the NAACP's Roy Wilkins, whom a King friend would describe as "psychotic about Martin," was sharply suspicious of this messianic young Southern preacher who might set loose an unmanageable new popular force into the accustomed order of things.

Meanwhile, King's SCLC remained a rather scrappy and flimsy affair, kept gaspingly alive only by the exertions of a former NAACP field organizer and veteran civil rights campaigner named Ella Baker. Almost always in financial extremis, with no consistent source of subsidy beyond King's speaking fees, it operated out of a dumpy little office on Atlanta's Auburn Avenue with only the most meager staff. One of them happened to be Bob Moses, a quiet and bespectacled youth out of Harlem with a Harvard master's in philosophy, who, gentle, withdrawn, whispery voiced, devoted to reading Camus, was virtually a pure mystic and was to become, in the heats and savageries of Mississippi in a few years, something like the movement's alter-saint to King.

Through this makeshift beginning time, the SCLC mostly reflected King's own scatter of attentions, its efforts at voter registration desultory, indulging in sporadic spasms of impressively nomenclatured but ultimately evanescent organizing, like an Institute for Nonviolent Resistance to Segregation, fancies of training a "nonviolent army" of volunteers for deployment to sites of developing confrontation — if any could ever be made to develop. For the time being, the SCLC seemed occupied chiefly in issuing a steady volley of bravura press communiqués.

During this long winter of fretful unconsummation, King had also bent to putting together, in collaboration with Stanley Levison, the first of his several books, a personal memoir of the Montgomery campaign to be titled *Stride Toward Freedom*. But its progress, with King's far-flung scamper of other endeavors, was wayward and erratic, King contributing mostly snatches of material that Levison labored to structure into something readable, at times writing whole passages himself, which King readily and thankfully accepted. Other stretches of the book were composed from the suggestions of advisers like Bayard Rustin — and, it was found years later, from King's wholesale and unacknowledged smugglings, as with his school papers and doctoral thesis, from the texts of others. Actually, it had long been a preacherly tradition in both black and white pulpits to rustle ideas and passages and even the whole herd of a sermon from other ministers. But more, for all his enormous powers in the popular physics of oratory, writing itself, that different element of talking on paper, was never King's forte. And if he still seemed oblivious to scholarly punctilios, it no doubt owed to his feeling caught up in the far more consequential exertion of acting as leader of a movement struggling to rise: what possessed him was not writing but creating history. But Levison, hardly able to argue any of these extratextual considerations to the book's publisher, strove to salvage it from successive editing emergencies — a pattern that would be repeated with all King's subsequent books.

Then, in the midst of this time of frenetically casting about for some way to continue the moral glory of Montgomery, King was ambushed by a warrant for his extradition back to that city, in a last swipe at him by Alabama's rancorous segregationist governor, John Patterson, to face charges of lying on his 1956 and 1958 state tax returns — the first time Alabama had ever prosecuted anyone for perjury in his tax filings. King seemed stricken to the point of tears by the allegation that he had taken for himself unreported helpings of movement funds, protesting that while he had "no pretense to absolute goodness," if he had "one virtue, it's honesty." In the trial, the questioned deposits into his account were shown, from hastily scrawled entries in his diary during the time, to be obvious reimbursements for expenses in his movement activities, and the jury was obliged to return a verdict of not guilty. But the episode had plunged King into an uncommon misery, "caused him more suffering," Coretta would remember, "than any other event of his life up to that point." Particularly coming at this tenuous pass for his movement ministry, it was exactly the sort of accusation, of a crude, petty venality — arising out of the cynicism that he had to be after something other than what he was preaching — that always had a way of especially blighting his spirit.

This little tribulation had befallen King, as it happened, several months after he had found himself arrested for the third time in Montgomery, though under somewhat more whimsical circumstances than before. He had returned to lend encouragement to Ralph Abernathy in his embarrassment at having to testify in the trial, prosecuted by local law officials with a vigor close to glee, of a man who had assaulted Abernathy in his church office for, the man claimed, regularly frisking with his wife — the infuriated husband pursuing Abernathy out of the church and down the street for two blocks with a hatchet. But when King sought to enter the courtroom with Abernathy, two policemen curtly notified him that only Abernathy could be admitted, and when King objected, they seized him and wrestled him along the corridor, his arm wrenched up behind his back, to the booking desk, where he was charged with loitering. News photos of King's gratuitously violent handling provoked an outcry that mostly disregarded the burlesque matter of Abernathy's mortification that had brought him there.

But in fact, King himself was now undergoing, more discreetly and quietly, a not dissimilar discomfiture of his own.

Already, dismays were being whispered about within quarters of the black community regarding King's sexual corsairing in his coursings about the country. One black newspaper in Pittsburgh even printed an advisory that "a movement minister in the deep South, a man who has been making the headlines recently in his fight for civil rights, had better watch his step," warning that his segregationist antagonists were bent on "catching the preacher in a hotel room with a woman other than his wife." A Los Angeles minister was concerned enough to write King, cautioning about his gambols with women who "too often delight in the satisfaction they get out of affairs with men of unusual prominence. Enemies are not above using them to a man's detriment. White women can be lures. You must exercise more care." Indeed, King, with his tremendous soul-vitality pent within a kind of flowery courtliness, had come to attract everywhere he went swimmings of avid females, black and white, who would slip him notes — one aide remembered a suburban reception with "women making passes at Martin Luther King I could not believe. . . . They would walk up to him and they would sort of lick their lips and hint." And to be sure, King "loved beautiful women," associates would later testify; "he really was just interested in *women,* period." Abernathy was later to recount that sometimes, as the two of them were sitting on the rostrum at a meeting, King would lean to him and mutter, "You see that woman giving me the eye, the one in the red dress?"

In truth, there's no question any longer that his gusto for libidinous adventure was voracious. To an acquaintance who urged on him more restraint, he replied, "I'm away from home twenty-five to twenty-seven days a month," and, as he put it with a smacking bluntness, "Fucking's a form of anxiety reduction." Throughout his one-night scrimmagings on the road, he also kept up a series of more intense involvements, often several simultaneously. Even Abernathy, not precisely disinclined himself to indulgences of the flesh, would eventually warn King that he had allowed a particular affair with a young woman to become recklessly conspicuous. But King responded, "Ralph, what you say may be right, but I don't care. . . . I have no intention of cutting off this relationship." All such admonitions about his liaisons he rebuffed as stoutly as he had the warnings about his interracial romance while a seminary student at Crozer. It was as if he was resolved, this time, to compensate for his loss of that love by pitching himself heedlessly into a kind of Dionysian abandon of sensual carnival.

Yet all the while, he could never stop agonizing, often in homiletic disguise in public, over what he felt to be this dire dichotomy within him, lamenting to college audiences and his own church congregation that "each of us is something of a schizophrenic personality, we're split up and divided against ourselves. There is something of a civil war going on within all our lives," that "within the best of us there is some evil, and within the worst of us there is some good. . . . All of us know somehow there is a Mr. Hyde and Dr. Jekyll in us." Though his congregations could hardly have suspected how fully they were serving King as sacramental recipient for his own confessionals, he would call out, "Many of you here know something of what it is to struggle with sin. . . . It may have been slavery to drink, untruthfulness, the impurity of selfishness or sexual promiscuity. And as the years unfolded, the vice grew bolder and bolder. . . . You knew all along that it was wrong and that it had invaded your life as an unnatural intruder," but "the evil was still with you, God would not cast it out."

King's compulsion to lubricious binges would not be all that different, actually, from the disposition of many popular visionaries who have made themselves out of, come to operate on, the power of their passions. But with King, one senses, it was from the tension of this inner dichotomy between spirit and flesh that much of his momentous public force derived. More, there was about King no slight hint that he somehow felt, in his oldest moral workings, that he must continually experience sin to continuously know the soul-regenerating wonder of forgiveness and redemption — or as Taylor Branch endeavors to nicely cast it, "It was better to overcome the siren music of evil by listening to the melodies of Orpheus than by stuffing wax into one's ears." In another connection once, remarking on the racist violence of some whites, King proposed that while guilt had "a constructive angle, and that is, it causes you to repent . . . mend your evil," it can also impel one to "drown the guilt by engaging more in the very act that brought the guilt." In this way, it may not be too fanciful to suggest, King — in a variant of Martin Luther's own precept "Sin boldly, but believe and rejoice in Christ more boldly still" — was driven to crucify himself over and over again on a cross of guilt with his secret licentiousness in order to renew his soul with the experience of yet another resurrection into grace and restoration to his high calling. And the greater his need, as his embattlement would mount over the years, for that renewal of spiritual power, the deeper became his descents into the prodigality that would produce it.

Even so, one interior toll of all this, as King once admitted to a confidant, was that "I am conscious of two Martin Luther Kings," the figure of popular veneration seeming "somebody foreign to me." In all, he confessed, "there's a kind of dualism in my life." Actually, a polyality of conflicts was more the case. In private with his closest comrades, often over hefty drinks, King would also give himself over to a profane, Rabelaisian bawdiness, guffawing at Abernathy about his own lickerish misadventure that had landed him in the Montgomery court trial. But a corollary guilt harrying King, ever since his conscription by accident into leadership of the movement in Montgomery, had continued to be a sense of personal inadequacy to the mission into which he had been lofted — that, as Stanley Levison would later reflect, he had merely wound up "an actor in history at a particular moment that called for a personality, and he had simply been selected as that personality. . . . If he had been less humble, he could have lived with this kind of acclaim, but because he was genuinely a man of humility, he really couldn't live with it." One SCLC operative later observed that much of King's torment came from trying to carry "this absolutely duplicitous role or posture," that "when he represented black America, he had to stand up there like a man of iron, the man of perfection, which he certainly wasn't."

King accordingly became increasingly haunted by Gandhi and what he took to praising as his "absolute self-discipline," in which "there was no gulf between the public and private." However illusionary that image, King was endlessly aspiring to a Gandhian kind of self-abnegation himself, straining to keep to, in place of Gandhi's fasts and loincloths and spinning wheel, at least a semblance of austerity in how he lived. This compulsion toward a Gandhian modesty also meant always having to strive against his own flushes of vanity, his hankerings for notability and consequence — he once had the SCLC actually issue a press release announcing he'd been invited to address an assembly at Harvard — and he was always edgy about anyone discovering how substantially his books were the work of others.

Before long, in place of his customary spruceness of attire — his fastidious attention to his appearance complicated by a tough beard that required daily applications of a rank depilatory paste to remove, scraped off with a knife — Coretta and others close to King began to notice he seemed strangely neglectful of his dress, unmindful that his suits might be rumpled, his shirts a bit frowsy at the edges. In another sign of a growing unease about his fitness to be hailed as the black American successor to Gandhi, he once blurted to Coretta, "I don't want to keep any property, I don't need a house." Nevertheless, under her entreaties, he finally consented to move, with their four children now, from their small rented house to a more spacious residence; but this new home "troubled him greatly," Levison remembered. He even pronounced to Coretta at one point that "a man who dedicates himself to a cause doesn't need a family," that anyone who's given up his life to serving all humankind must neglect his own household to an extent that would be appalling in anyone else.

Such professions Coretta did not receive with total equanimity. Increasingly there were little sizzlings of distemper between them, Coretta not concealing her resentment when he'd fail to phone from his latest rambling to check on the children, or when she learned, often from others, that he would not be including her in such auspicious occasions as visits to the White House. As intense and soulfully ambitious a woman as ever, she had not reckoned on things turning out precisely this way back during his flamboyant courtship of her in Boston, when she'd finally abandoned her hopes of becoming a concert soloist to share a life with him in some larger calling, or when they'd been whirled up out of their snug situation in Montgomery into the giddy unfoldings of the movement. Aides accompanying King in his peregrinations about the country now began hearing bitter phone fracases with Coretta in Atlanta about his ever more protracted absences from home.

But beyond delicately acknowledging once that "my husband was what psychologists might call a guilt-ridden man," Coretta had simply resolved to remain impervious to the intimations reaching her of King's romantic caperings, maintaining with a dauntless ethereality that "all that other business just doesn't have a place in the very high level relationship we enjoyed." In fact, long before Memphis, she had already come to be accomplished in the loneliness of an apprentice widowhood. Even so, whatever her disappointments over all that had intruded since their beginnings together, when King once phoned her from an airport after having missed a flight, exhausted and in another eclipse of despair about being surrounded by adversity and failings of faith everywhere, Coretta told him, "*I* believe in you, if that means anything." That was to wind up in the end about all left to her — to believe in him.

Meanwhile, in his restless forgings about through those distracted years after Montgomery, King had nevertheless gradually gathered around him that inner company of lieutenants who would come to be called King's Horsemen in the campaigns ahead. There was already, of course, the dutiful Abernathy, his baggy, dolorous-faced, waggish Sancho Panza, totally steadfast, whom King, shortly after moving to Atlanta, had arranged to bring over with him by finding a church there for him to pastor. Abernathy's devotion to King was never difficult to divine: far more humbly educated, he would later admit "how dull your own company is and how much you depend on the existence of others to give meaning and color to your life." But Abernathy's peculiar place as King's closest crony, this tubby jester disposed to slump into a doze during SCLC meetings, never ceased to baffle and exasperate almost everyone else, the more so when King made it known that should he ever be eliminated, Abernathy was to succeed him as president of the SCLC. It was as if Abernathy, as no one else quite could, somehow always kept King in comfortable touch with the simpler, earthier, more commonplace savors of life, refreshing King with his mere presence. He would bring King on at mass meetings with a country cornbread drollness that was a perfect counterpoint to King's loftier intonations. "I was always good at warming up audiences for him," he would later fondly reminisce. "I was always good at tellin' jokes and bein' humorous and all that, you know." But it was also Abernathy who would be most frequently jailed with King, hanging faithfully at his side right up to the motel balcony in Memphis.

In time, there also came on with King a young minister from the National Council of Churches, Andrew Young, who was everything Abernathy was not — urbane, deftly discerning, suavely articulate, having grown up in the pale-coffee gentility of the black community in New Orleans as the son of an affluent dentist. His temperately realistic counsel King was to listen to as carefully as Levison's, until it came to be widely supposed Young would most likely be King's natural successor. Eventually, King brought in as the SCLC's executive director Wyatt T. Walker, a whip-tense, imperiously assertive preacher from Petersburg, Virginia, who happily described himself as King's administrative "son of a bitch," declaring, "One big piece of evidence about the greatness of Martin Luther King is that a man as vain as I am is willing to play second fiddle to him." Joining King later was a Birmingham preacher of an equally autocratic temperament, Fred Shuttlesworth, and yet another Baptist minister, C. T. Vivian, with his own roosterish audacity. Later would come Hosea Williams, from Savannah, a burly figure with the hoarse-voiced, hot urgency of some Third World bush fighter, whom King indeed liked to call "my wild man, my Castro."

But perhaps the most mystically intense and byzantine of them all was James Bevel, originally out of the Mississippi Delta, with simmering pitchblende eyes in a tawny, vaguely Mongolian face, commonly out-fitted in crumpled denim coveralls and, on his glassily shaved head, an embroidered skullcap in reverence for the Hebrew prophets, who when jailed with other demonstrators, would pass his time preaching to them in inexhaustible, well-nigh Blakean transports. King in later years would suspect at times that Bevel was actually crazy, and in truth, he seemed to inhabit some remote margin of reality where he was always in danger of being electrocuted by his own metaphysical genius. Despite that, as one SCLC aide would recall, Bevel always "had a very uncanny way of making an impact on Martin."

It was Bevel, as it happened, who would eventually bring into the SCLC, late into the Southern phase of its movement, a towering, hefty, sweepingly eager youth from Greenville, South Carolina, now a seminary student in Chicago, with no slight swashbuckling flair of his own — Jesse Jackson. The youngest of King's aides, Jackson would go on to direct one of the few measurably successful SCLC programs, Operation Breadbasket, a campaign for economic integration through bringing more blacks into inner-city businesses all the way up to executive levels. Already with a certain incandescent promise and overlarge presence, Jackson would eventually be regarded by King with some ambivalence, both a fascination and disquiet about his proud, impatient hungers.

But then, this whole motley assortment of personalities around King — Young, Walker, Vivian, Shuttlesworth, Williams, Bevel, others with them like Bernard Lee and Bernard Lafayette — made up a tempestuously virtuoso lot: to some associates, King "seemed to assemble every egocentric character in America." They were as well a raunchy troupe for the most part, some roistering outrageously at times among whatever likely young ladies were at hand — the movement generally, for that matter, was hardly "a sour-faced, pietistic" adventure, one veteran has since attested; "everybody was out getting laid." And when collected together of an evening, sweaty and weary, stripped down to their shorts and gulping beer in some frumpish hotel room out in the violence-muggy weathers of another field of confrontation, they would belabor each other with railleries about respective pomposities and peccadilloes. Also warring with each other continuously in their work for King, chronically threatening to resign, they constituted a more or less running free-for-all of egos, "almost all of them self-styled prophets with a kind of messianism," recalls Andrew Young, "but that's what it took. Martin always said, Look, normal people don't challenge the law of the land, you got to be creatively maladjusted. We need people who'll trouble the waters." As often, though, the waters they seemed intent on troubling were each other's. "*Nobody* got along," remembers Young — who himself once slugged Hosea Williams for suggesting he was an Uncle Tom "plant" by the FBI. Williams later acknowledged that some staff meetings would devolve into members slinging chairs at each other, and one former SCLC associate has marveled that at times the staff would "damn near crawl across the table and slit each other's throats." Meanwhile, King abided this ongoing donnybrook with a seemingly supernatural patience. He was not unaware that "all these strong egos, all of them with their own stories to tell," in Young's words, were each "in some way, maybe subconsciously, wishing that he was Martin Luther King," and at one time or another, says Young, they all considered that "Martin Luther King was going too slow." King was "so calm, mild-mannered, soft-spoken, extremely logical and analytical about everything, that almost everybody would get constantly upset. Typically, brash young men mistake humility for weakness," and, Young goes on, "everybody thought they could one-up him, manipulate him, co-opt him for their own purposes. And he'd never fight back. It was almost as though he felt he had to let us do all that, and somehow in this neurotic mix he could find the final formula for continuing the movement."

II

But even while King was ranging about for another defining offensive like Montgomery, the Black Awakening begun there had been uncontainably amplifying over the South, beyond the purview of any single civil rights organization. The student lunch counter sit-ins had ramified rapidly into demonstrations in hundreds of cities and towns against segregated public facilities, jails filling with young protesters. In Nashville, Jim Lawson, long a Gandhian devotee, conducted workshops in mass nonviolent resistance that led to the fabled student sit-in movement there.

King was not long in recognizing the import of this surge of eager young black cadres into the movement. To accommodate it, out of an SCLC student conference in 1960 at Shaw University in Raleigh, North Carolina, was born the Student Nonviolent Coordinating Committee (SNCC), to act as a kind of commando strike force for deep-country operations. A seminary student in Nashville and a fervent acolyte of King's would eventually become its chairman: John Lewis, a stolid, stocky, surpassingly sweet-souled fellow out of the remotest back reaches of rural Alabama, who as a boy had wrestled with his thick stutter by preaching to the chickens on his family's farm.

But for all King's expansive hopes, there was from the start a divide of temperament between King's SCLC and most of SNCC's hot young militants, many of them with a suspicion of what seemed King's overly deliberate middle-class moderation and a lesser regard for the nonviolent ethic itself, taking it as merely a limited tactic for the moment. Inevitably, they were soon to detach themselves from any formal affiliation with the SCLC.

The growing dissonance of style and sensibility between them crackled into the open during the Freedom Rides of 1961, when integrated parties of young blacks and their white compatriots (one not incidental revolution worked by the movement was that white college students from privileged families were now applying to join its black youths as followers) set out into the inner reaches of the South on bus journeys that soon turned into gauntlets of mayhem from vigilante mobs along the way — one bus burned outside Anniston, Alabama; a pack of white marauders swarming with lead pipes and baseball bats over riders on their arrival at the bus station in Montgomery. A congregation that had gathered in Abernathy's church there in support of the Freedom Rides, with King having flown in for the rally as well, found themselves trapped in the sanctuary through a long night of bombarding rocks and bricks from an enormous white mob howling outside. King retreated to the church's basement at one point to place pleading calls for help to Attorney General Robert Kennedy, declaring the church could soon be set afire. Kennedy crisply assured him of federal attention to the problem (but mused dryly afterward, "He rather berated me for what was happening to him at the time"). It was dawn before the mob had thinned away enough to allow those inside the church to leave, though still under National Guard escort. But when the students then appealed to King to join them in continuing their Freedom Ride on into Mississippi — "Where is your *body?*" — King awkwardly declined, explaining that he was still technically under probation from an earlier arrest in Georgia. The fearfulness of that experience for him made the prospect of winding up in a Mississippi jail all the more unnerving, and caused him finally to blurt out, in a desperate defensiveness whose gaucherie stunned the students, "I think I should choose the time and place of my Golgotha."

Early the next morning, when students began boarding the bus to Mississippi, King was there, standing by the bus's door, to wave them on with an emotional blessing flushed with guilt and regret. But his performance on the whole had only deepened the disillusionment with him among the movement's younger militants. John Lewis, who had himself been bloodily battered at the Montgomery bus station, would remember, more ruefully than bitterly, that "it was a big criticism that he came to the bus station and saw the other people off and he refused to go." Many of those leaving on the bus that morning, in fact, and more after them, were to end up in the dungeon keep of Mississippi's Parchman Penitentiary. King was left in a self-torturing remorse about that for long afterward. But one likely source of his reluctance to accompany the riders into imprisonment in Mississippi was that he had already served his own turn in a similar hell.

The previous fall, when young activists in Atlanta had importuned him with challenges of how he could remain a leader of the movement if he himself refused to risk jail with them, King had finally agreed to join them in a sit-in at a downtown department store's segregated lunchroom — for which he and some thirty-five other demonstrators were promptly arrested and delivered into the county jail. But it had apparently slipped King's mind that he happened to be on probation for an incidental traffic offense several months earlier, and now, for violating the terms of that probation with his sit-in arrest, he was swiftly ordered to serve a four-month sentence at hard labor. At three-thirty in the morning, he was roughly awakened in his cell in the county jail, shackled into leg irons and handcuffs, taken out and toppled into the back of a police car. Then, with no indication of destination, he was driven for two hours through the night to, emerging in the early dawn light, the hulking complex of Georgia's gothic Reidsville Penitentiary, where he was locked alone in a cell. It was the horror again of his first arrest in Montgomery, only now, in the famously barbarous Reidsville, of more terrifying proportions. He would admit afterward that he had broken into weeping in his cell, while swept with shame at this weakness in himself.

King's internment in Reidsville had taken place, as it happened, during the finishing heats of the 1960 presidential contest between Vice President Richard Nixon and Senator John Kennedy, and Coretta now frantically phoned a congenial contact in the Kennedy campaign, Harris Wofford, to plead, "They are going to kill him, I know they are going to kill him. . . ." Wofford managed to get word of what had happened to Kennedy, who quickly phoned Coretta in Atlanta to assure her of his concern about her husband, telling her to let him know directly if there was some way he might help. Considerably more exercised when he learned of King's jailing was Robert Kennedy, who impetuously phoned the sentencing judge directly to tartly complain about how King had been treated. The judge, an obscure county magistrate in a still predominantly Democratic state, finding himself now suddenly caught up in a presidential campaign, shortly determined that King could be released on bail after all while his case was being appealed. But when King finally emerged from the depths of Reidsville, he wore a look of shaken fragility described by one surprised and moved white Southern reporter, who'd never seen him before, as a "vulnerability . . . not softness, naiveté, but somehow hurtable."

King would always have the good instinct as a social evangel to keep himself at a remove from any direct political enlistment — from ever transferring what was for him a spiritual vision into, as it were, the power machineries of Caesar. As he would explain in later years when he was himself being suggested as a peace candidate for president, "I have come to think of my role as one which operates outside the realm of partisan politics . . . as a conscience of all the parties and all the people." Accordingly, at the outset of the 1960 presidential competition between Nixon and Kennedy, he had stipulated that he could not properly endorse either candidate, and now, despite gaining release from Reidsville by the intercession of the Kennedys, in the days afterward he

117

still insisted it would be inappropriate for him to declare for either contender. But he did not abstain from observing that "I am grateful to Senator Kennedy for the genuine concern he expressed in my arrest," and while Nixon had let it be known that he would refrain from any comment on King's situation, the Democratic candidate, King now noted, had "exhibited moral courage of a high order." Daddy King, however, was not even that circuitous: though a Republican all his life, he sturdily trumpeted that, for what Kennedy had done for his son, he would now be voting for him — "I've got all my votes, and I've got a suitcase, and I'm going to take them up there and dump them in his lap" — even if he was a Catholic. (Which would later elicit the wry remark from Kennedy to Wofford, "Imagine Martin Luther King having a bigot for a father," and then with a little smile, "Well, we all have fathers, don't we?")

But it was enough, even absent an outright endorsement from King, for the Kennedy campaign to let loose a blizzard of leaflets titled " 'No Comment' Nixon Versus a Candidate with a Heart, Senator Kennedy" to black churches over the nation the Sunday before the election. It was not without significance, then, that in Kennedy's subsequent hangnail-close win in the election, which would have been reversed by the slightest shift of votes in, say, Texas and Illinois, the African American vote had swung from 3–2 Republican in 1956 to 7–3 Democratic in 1960. Eisenhower himself grumped afterward that the outcome had been decided by those "couple of phone calls" by the Kennedy brothers on King's behalf.

In the end, the entire affair, from the Kennedys' calls in the first place to their effect on the election of America's next president, was a remarkable affirmation, despite his uneventful float since Montgomery, of King's singular stature still as the great symbolic tribune of the Black Awakening for America's black citizenry. Somehow, in the intensity of his sheer presence, his solemn carriage and Isaianic oratory, he touched something in their souls beyond all conventional measuring or analysis. At one of his voter registration rallies in a scanty little Mississippi settlement, an elderly black man reported that he had walked thirteen miles there just to personally behold him.

But the Kennedy brothers themselves, despite their intervention to get him released from Reidsville, were never really to com-

prehend, throughout most of their administration, that full meaning of King. It became
instead the immemorial conflict between
prophet and princes, a relationship for the
most part of mutual estrangement. The
president and his brother were, to begin
with, possessed of a relentless caution of political calibration, particularly now given the
electoral tenuousness of their governing authority, and they were hardly unwitting that
King constituted the most sinister sort of
hobgoblin to the standing political estate in
the South. Too, however wondrous his
apostleship in the Montgomery movement,
King yet seemed too specialized and parochial a figure, just a young Southern black
preacher still tossing about for some sequel
to that sensation of four years ago, to carry
any serious national political heft. Accordingly, right after the election, King was invited neither for a personal session with the
incoming president, as were other, more
regulation black leaders like Roy Wilkins,
nor even finally to Kennedy's inauguration
itself. Nor was he asked to the large convocation not long afterward of civil rights emi-
nences in the office of Attorney General
Robert Kennedy.

From the same close political circum-
spections, the new president had also calcu-

lated that the humor of Congress and the nation generally would be impossibly inhospitable to any substantial civil rights legislation for a good while yet. King, though relegated now to a solitary voice on the fringes of official relevance, nevertheless began sounding alarms that Kennedy was betraying promises made to the nation's black community, including a commitment to an executive order eliminating segregation in all federally aided housing, that had brought him his electoral margin of victory. At last then, nine months after the election, King was granted a personal meeting with the president at the White House. He did not exactly dispel Kennedy's misgivings about him with his exhortations on what had become an obsession with him: for Kennedy to issue a "Second Emancipation Proclamation" that would abolish with a single executive order, as Lincoln had slavery one hundred years before, all segregation in the country — a proposition Kennedy received with, at best, a bemused politeness. King personally struck both Kennedy brothers, in fact, as something of an oddity: unexpectedly mild and deferential, with a certain preacherly heaviness of tone, but finally inscrutable, a man perhaps of a kind of holy gullibility.

It was to be an abiding gap of natures between them. King confided to Harris Wofford, who was now working in Robert Kennedy's Justice Department, that the president "had the understanding and political skill, but so far the moral passion is lacking." But "moral passion" was precisely what the Kennedy brothers had a pronounced allergy to — the potentially disastrous naiveté of King's sort of missionary idealism. To their brisk, taut, ironic style, King was too earnest, too "hot" — he simply didn't fit their sensibilities. Even on through the high struggle of Birmingham, he was to remain a figure whose real meaning was beyond their ken.

Not only King, for that matter, but the movement itself in its pell-mell expansion seemed a force largely beyond their range of understanding. In one off-the-record conversation with a deputation of black newspaper editors, President Kennedy had wishfully submitted that he could see no real divide between blacks and whites in the country. With their devotion to the regular mechanisms of the system, the Kennedys did contract an enthusiasm for voter registration as an acceptably orderly civil rights effort, and Robert Kennedy's Justice Department quietly collaborated in the formation of a voter registration program, funded by private institutions, called the Voter Education Project, a coalition operation of the major civil rights organizations at the time. Voter registration, to the Kennedys' minds, was the proper political answer from which all other blessings would then methodically flow. But beyond that, neither the president nor his brother could quite understand so much being so histrionically made of such (to them) mundane matters as equal access to bathroom facilities, who should be admitted to sit where in a movie theater, have their hair cut by whom. During the turmoil of the Freedom Rides, Robert Kennedy, in a testy phone exchange with King in Montgomery after King's call from the basement of the besieged church, had urged a "cooling-off period" in this riotously provocative challenge to the laws segregating bus travel, and King retorted that "our conscience tells us that the law is wrong and we must resist." RFK, taking that as a threat from King to prolong the crisis with its jailings of protesters refusing bail, snapped, "The fact that they stay in jail is not going to have the slightest effect on me." King, himself offended by this rejoinder, indicated that hundreds of thousands more students just might come down to join the Freedom

Rides, and Kennedy shot back, "Don't make statements that sound like a threat. That's not the way to deal with us." Afterward, Kennedy indicated his foggy fix on the phenomenon breaking out around him when he expostulated to an aide about the mounting numbers taking part in the Freedom Rides, "Do you know that one of them is against the atom bomb?" and later complained that it was all "good propaganda for America's enemies."

As it was soon to turn out, though, Kennedy would feel constrained to ask the Interstate Commerce Commission to banish segregation from all aspects and facilities of interstate travel, whether bus, train, or plane. In fact, while they scarcely realized it as yet, the Kennedys themselves had come to be impressed by King and his movement into what would prove, however grudging and halting, their own pilgrimage of conscience.

Ominously, though, King had by now drawn the cold watchful eye of J. Edgar Hoover, the longtime Grand Inquisitor of the FBI — this largely a consequence of King's enduring closeness to Stanley Levison, whom FBI intelligence had concluded, with his financial support of the

Communist Party since the forties, was a member of the Party himself. Actually, with King's abrupt ascent into a national notability during the Montgomery campaign, he would already have stirred an alarmed alertness in Hoover, given to a Coolidge-era perspective about blacks in general, as a figure posing a danger of racial distemper in the country. Then, in 1959, when King had addressed a civil rights youth rally in Washington organized by A. Philip Randolph, Hoover glimpsed a mention in an FBI report that Randolph had paid thanks for logistical assistance in the event to Levison. This connection now of Levison to King rang in Hoover's mind the possibility that King, either unknowingly or willingly, was operating under Communist management. Then, after Kennedy's inauguration, Hoover's attention was called to a passing suggestion by King in a magazine essay that "if the FBI were integrated, many persons who now defy federal law might come under restraints from which they are presently free." Even so incidental a plaint about his sacrosanct Bureau from the likes of King was, for Hoover, an intolerably slanderous impudence.

While King still had no inkling of it, there had in fact commenced what was to become a prolonged shadow war between him and Hoover. Though it would take place mostly out of the public eye, the two of them were to be locked into an elemental conflict as figures reflecting — more, virtually embodying — two poles of the American character: that ethic lasting from Plymouth's starch-collared society of probity, discipline, righteousness as a matter of a ruthless cleanliness of behavior, this rectitudinousness in schizophrenic tension with an unrulier urge lasting from the frontier, a restlessness with authority and convention, a readiness for adventure in exploring the farther, windy moral opens of life. Since assuming power as director of the FBI in 1924, Hoover had not appreciably changed his notion of what should be the character of the nation — sedate, sober, orderly, and properly segregated, like his FBI — and he had ever since applied all the energies of the institution he had created to keeping it that way, to preserve the plainer America of his nostalgias against alien contamination and the subversions of more diverse cultural weathers. By the fifties, he had become for much of the country — this stubby, pluggish, stern little pug-bull of a man with a cauliflower pallor and flat, blunt face — a kind of totem figure of law and uprightness.

In the process, he had consolidated the FBI into perhaps Washington's greatest private preserve of official power ever, his intelligence files holding even many in the halls of government in fear.

His own father had been a failed bureaucrat who died of what a doctor listed as "melancholia." Hoover had continued to live with his mother until he was forty-three, when she died. He never once traveled beyond the boundaries of the United States, demanded the same hotel room each year on his vacations, had his agents make sure it was at a precise temperature before he arrived. Each morning in Washington when he came down to breakfast, if the poached egg awaiting him was not of a certain consistency, he would instantly send it back to the kitchen for another to be prepared — which sometimes, after a mere taste, he would then place on the floor for his dog. He never married. His long companionship with his associate director Clyde Tolson, with whom he had lunch and dinner every day, gave strong reason for the subsequent conjecture that Hoover was at least a suppressed homosexual, but the greater likelihood seems that, with his congenital, fanatic aversion to deviations of any kind from the norm, he was actually asexual: neuter.

Given all this, it's no surprise that something about King from the very beginning provoked an almost biological aversion in Hoover. After then discovering King's close association with Stanley Levison, Hoover rapidly notified Robert Kennedy that King's most intimate counselor was very likely a Communist agent manipulating him. Though entertaining a wary distaste of their own for Hoover, the Kennedy brothers, not without a sense of King's special import for black Americans, were considerably dismayed by the director's claims. They agreed to Hoover's initiating electronic surveillance of Levison. But they also elected, without letting King know of that surveillance, to advise him privately about the intelligence on Levison, though only in general terms, and to warn him he should immediately terminate such a hugely risky relationship. They also protested the SCLC's employment of a yet more dubious individual, Jack O'Dell, a young black installed by Bayard Rustin and Levison in the SCLC's New York office to direct its fundraising mailings, whom the FBI flatly maintained was a still active member of the Communist Party.

King was left not a little unsettled by these dire tidings relayed to him with such a sepulchral air of emergency. But, assured by both Levison and O'Dell they no longer had any affiliation whatever with the Party, King, to the profound consternation of the Kennedys, dismissed the admonitions from the Justice Department, maintaining that without more proof than such broad-stroke allegations, he could not honorably discard anyone, whatever their political past, who was now devotedly serving the movement — especially so intrepid a friend as Levison. But King's resistance only confirmed for the Kennedys his sanctimonious, potentially calamitous naiveté. While it all may have owed as much to King's notorious sluggishness whenever faced by painful staff-cutting exigencies, his dogged reluctance to separate from Levison was to persist as a trouble-somely murky business, raising questions about King's capacity, with his own socialist political sensibility, for appreciating the hazardous implications of Levison's Communist connections. But it finally came down to a human matter of loyalty for King.

Meanwhile, as the civil rights struggle kept escalating, the Kennedy administration — caught in the crisis over the admission of James Meredith to the University of

Mississippi, the confrontation with a rankly defiant Alabama governor George Wallace over the admission of two black students to the university there, the outbreak eventually of King's offensive in Birmingham — was finally compelled into a commitment to the movement, to the extent of presenting to Congress a bill to eliminate segregation in public accommodations. Thus it was that President Kennedy took King for a private stroll in the Rose Garden and, placing a hand on his shoulder, murmured almost offhandedly, "I assume you know you're under close surveillance," and proceeded to somberly notify him that he absolutely must break from Levison and O'Dell: "They're both Communists. You've got to get rid of them." By risking disclosure of his continuing association with them, Kennedy warned, King was gravely jeopardizing not only his own leadership, but the whole movement, and "if they shoot *you* down, they'll shoot us down too." King allowed that he would offer no argument on O'Dell, but he still demurred on Levison: "I know Stanley, and I can't believe this." Until he could see conclusive evidence that Levison was actually working as a Communist agent, King protested, he could not throw him over simply on such unsubstantiated imputations coming from a source like Hoover.

Continuing FBI scrutiny of Levison discovered he was assisting King on another book, and Hoover now began insisting to the attorney general that, owing to King's refusal to disconnect from this certain Communist operative, it had become a national security imperative to expand the wiretapping to include King himself. Though acutely uncomfortable about the possibilities of grotesque scandal in such a measure, Robert Kennedy was also aware that Hoover was making this demand with an even more ghastly threat behind it.

Ever since Hoover had first begun relaying confidential investigative reports on political figures for Franklin Roosevelt's private delectation, the services offered by Hoover had always posed a special temptation for those who ruled in Washington — an informal symbiosis in which he was to become much the creation of the men he served. But within the great vault of power he had so constructed for himself, Hoover had made provisions that nothing, short of the hand of God, would ever likely dislodge him. Over the decades he had also been compiling a second, even more secret set of files on the mighty of Washington themselves, from congressmen to presidents, which provided him ample capital to assure his survival. Included in those files, Hoover had not neglected to apprise the Kennedy White House, was intelligence about Jack Kennedy's dalliances with Judith Campbell, mistress of Chicago mob chieftain Sam Giancana, which held the most nightmarish implications of political calamity with Giancana's collaboration in a CIA plot for a Mafia assassination of Fidel Castro — and what was perhaps an even graver security concern, Kennedy's affair with a woman from East Germany who was strongly suspected of being a spy. It had not been lost on Robert Kennedy that Hoover had already contrived selective leaks to the press about Levison and O'Dell, and if word similarly got out, even just to certain congressmen, about these amours of the president's, the results, as Hoover knew Robert Kennedy knew, would be catastrophic. And as Hoover kept pressing him with demands for the King wiretap, Robert Kennedy at last assented. If he had not, he confessed sometime afterward to an aide, it would have meant "no living with the Bureau."

It wasn't long, then, before the Bureau's expanded electronic surveillance picked up King, in a conversation with a wiretapped friend, relaxing into one of his boisterous commentaries about more lascivious matters than Hoover could ever have imagined. With this serendipitous development, Hoover was certain he had his fatal hold on King — raw proof to Hoover, who never in his long career had been given to complex understandings of life and human character, that King was hardly the high social prophet he presented himself as, but all along merely a "tom cat," as he would later scribble on a memo, "with obsessive, degenerate sexual urges." And from now on, Hoover was to pursue King, though King was still not fully knowing of it, with the single-minded relentlessness of Inspector Javert tracking Jean Valjean.

III

But all that was still months ahead as, in the winter of 1961, King, increasingly overcast of spirit, was still lurching about trying to find some moment to follow Montgomery. Under the Voter Education Project, the SCLC had been at least temporarily galvanized by substantial grants for mounting a new voter registration campaign over the

South, with citizenship schools to train registration workers. But King's own role as a
movement leader was still running largely on
memory. And when at last he thought he
sighted the possibility of another grand and
definitive engagement like Montgomery, it
had in fact mostly been opened up to him by
the guerrilla activists of SNCC.

For months, SNCC field operatives had
been working quietly to condition a popular
readiness for a full confrontation with white
authorities in Albany, Georgia — a drab
little city in the state's southwest sunstruck
flatlands of cotton and peanut fields. The
long restlessness of discontent in its black
community had finally collected, with
SNCC's aid, into an organization called the
Albany Movement. But over the course of
early demonstrations and arrests, there had
proliferated perhaps an overamplitude of
demands — the desegregation of Albany's
bus and train stations, of libraries and parks
and medical services, as well as a halt to the
systematically brutish police treatment of
blacks and the exclusion of blacks from juries. The sheer profusion of these appeals,
though, amounted to poignant testimony in
itself to segregation's well-nigh totalitarian
grip on the life of blacks in the South.

But the Albany Movement had encountered a resistance from local officials as obdurate as that in Montgomery, employing the ruse of a constant shifting of authority among the mayor, the city commission, and Albany's police chief, Laurie Pritchett. For his part, Chief Pritchett — despite his look, with his heavy bulk and cigar always stuffed in his mouth, of the consummate caricature of a white Southern lawman — had a drawingly amiable, possumlike wiliness, in which he had determined to answer the demonstrations by "killin' 'em with kindness," as it was described by one appreciative local official.

These gambits had served to consistently balk the Albany Movement so far, and finally one of its leaders phoned Atlanta to ask that King and the SCLC come down — which, with a ready alacrity, they did. But in King's urgency for another moment of truth like Montgomery, it was with only the muzziest idea of the internal complications of the crisis into which he was pitching himself.

With ranklings about King's pontifical style already having set in among the movement's young irregulars, the SNCC detachment in Albany was not exactly enchanted that the SCLC had now been invited in. At the same time, many in the black community at large were still somewhat uneasy about an all-out assault on the city's white power system. More critically, through the series of earlier demonstrations, almost all available money for bailing out those arrested had been exhausted, with some three hundred demonstrators still in jail. What's more, Robert Kennedy, after the vexations of the Freedom Rides that past summer, had assumed a resolute "hands off" posture toward this developing new ruction in Albany, even pronouncing that any real resolution of racial antagonisms there would come only when "local leaders talk it out."

In all, then, King was moving full force into a situation that already held incipient elements of disaster.

Nevertheless, King was received into Albany at a mass meeting with roaring cheers, clapping, a booming of the movement chorus adapted from the old revival meeting "Amen" song of praise, *Free-dom . . . Free-dom . . . Free-dom. . . .* It was in fact during the Albany campaign that, whatever else, the movement's music was delivered into its full voice — the freedom anthems like "Ain't Gonna Let Nobody Turn Me Round," "Keep Your Eyes on the Prize," "We Shall Not Be Moved," "Which Side Are You

On?," and finally, from its genesis as a black gospel hymn carried into the labor movement during the forties, "We Shall Overcome." Dual mass meetings were often held at two churches facing each other across an avenue, with the two congregations choiring the same freedom hymn back and forth to each other, until it seemed both churches were lifted like arks from all the daily oppressive gravities of the earth and on up into the quiet evening sky into eternity with Abraham and Moses and the prophets and Jesus himself. . . . King would then take the pulpit, declaiming in his great belling voice, "How long will we have to suffer injustices? Not long, because the moral arc of the universe bends toward justice. How long? Not long! Because —" His voice then swallowed in another detonation of shouts, applause, stomping feet. It was not hard for him to believe that after a long and bleary stasis of four years, Montgomery had indeed magically returned.

Demonstrations proceeded for weeks at local lunch counters and the bus station café and the city's parks, mass marches moving in the winter's chill bleak weather through downtown Albany to its city hall, where in the by now familiar and almost ritualistic scenario, they would be met and herdingly placed under arrest by Chief Pritchett's men. But Pritchett conducted these exercises with an unfailingly amicable restraint that effectively muffled their potential for moral theater. At the same time, he had managed to beguile many of the national reporters who had come flurring into Albany with King by professing that he had himself studied King's philosophy of nonviolent militancy and had decided it would be met here in Albany with nonviolent law enforcement, which would stop mass protests against segregation only so far as they presented threats to the public order — which, of course, meant all of them. Later, when a respected black matron visiting her maid's daughter in the jail of a neighboring county was, though six months pregnant, beaten by the sheriff and his deputies, a riot roiled up in Albany's black section, bottles and rocks flinging through the air, and Pritchett cracked to reporters, "You see them nonviolent rocks?" — the reporters' delight at this drollery oblivious to the outrage that had provoked the eruption in the first place. Some of the white press found Pritchett so surprisingly engaging, in fact, that they entered in an intelligence complicity with him by letting him listen to their tape recordings of interviews with movement leaders.

Under this stratagem of an unprovocative but steady internment of protesters, the count of those arrested had long since exceeded the capacity of Albany's jails to contain them, and the overload was shipped for storage in the jails of surrounding counties, then confined in barns, holding pens, fenced-in pastures. King himself had been duly arrested in a demonstration shortly after his arrival in Albany and was transferred, with Abernathy, to the jail in nearby Americus for special keeping by the sheriff there, Fred Chappell, a studiously surly fellow with a splenetically bulb-eyed face, whom King afterward described as "the meanest man in the world." But King declared he would remain in his cell, refusing bail, until some agreement was reached in Albany on the grievances of its black citizens. In his absence, what black leaders were left to negotiate did manage to arrive at a tentative, minimal accord with the city for, first, the release of jailed protesters awaiting trial, and second, if there were no more demonstrations for thirty days, the formation of a biracial committee to consider reforms — though with no insurance that any actual deliberations would take place.

This nebulous arrangement produced the first critical short-circuiting of King's Albany campaign. Though it would have seemed a rather wheezy climax to his commitment there, King — out of his old trauma about being held captive in a Southern jail, especially now in the aggressively truculent custody of Sheriff Chappell — somewhat precipitously allowed himself to be bailed out, explaining, "I would not want to stand in the way of any meaningful negotiations." With demonstrations conditionally suspended, King returned to Atlanta to await the course of those negotiations — whereupon the city's officials quickly disavowed the whole understanding.

King had been masterfully snookered, national press reports terming it "a devastating loss of face" for him, "a stunning defeat." King himself acknowledged afterward, "I'm sorry I was bailed out. I didn't understand at the time what was happening. We thought the victory had been won. When we got out, we discovered it was all a hoax." The Albany Movement nevertheless lurched on with sporadic sit-ins and arrests through the next several months, on into the blaring heat of a southwest Georgia summer — when King at last returned to face trial on the arrest charges of the previous winter. He was expeditiously convicted and sentenced to either a fine or forty-five days in the city jail. Still mortified over his hastily premature departure from the cell in Americus, King chose jail, hoping it might redeem him for that earlier embarrassment while also reenergizing the fast-fading Albany campaign. But Pritchett, canny to the sensation King's jailing could still produce, arranged for him to be released a few days later, claiming that some anonymous black benefactor had paid his fine.

Glaringly outmaneuvered again, a distressed King vowed at a mass meeting that night that he would now remain in Albany until the city consented to the movement's appeals. In a subsequent conference with King and the local black leadership, Chief Pritchett surprisingly seemed to agree to just that. But shortly afterward, the city commissioners repudiated those concessions, and Pritchett himself then publicly announced that "there has been nothing of a settlement in reference to anything." For good measure, the mayor and city manager, in a visit to the home in nearby Columbus of a federal district judge of commonly known segregationist sentiments, obtained from him an injunction against any further demonstrations in Albany — which would about extinguish all that was left of the movement's prospects there.

King's dilemma now, which he was to face again three years later in Selma, was whether, to sustain the last faltering fortunes of the Albany campaign, he would defy that very federal authority on which the civil rights movement had relied as its only hope for overcoming incorrigibly segregationist local powers. But his hesitation about flouting the restraining order became yet another instance in the spreading disaffection with King among the young outriders of SNCC, some of whom in Albany, with black churches in surrounding counties being firebombed, had taken on a Franz Fanon fierceness, not disinclined to fancies of reproducing in southwest Georgia a variation of the Battle of Algiers. In a stormy session one Sunday evening in the backyard of a local black leader, they assailed King for his reluctance to defy the court order, proposing he was already an anachronism out of the black past in the South with all his Bible sermonizing and bourgeois cautions, and too preoccupied with his national station and with organizing the very spirit out of what must remain a spontaneous "people's movement." It rampaged on like this into the late, cricket-chittering night, until, as reported by Taylor Branch, one SNCC member who was a measure more sympathetic to King implored him, "We are at the point where you have to provide the leadership even for the Kennedys, as well as the movement. So let's go to jail, bro'. I'm gonna be going. We'll be there together. . . . Even you have got to grow a little bit more."

The truth was, even with all his failings and guilts and self-doubts through these past five years, King was still operating out of a vastness of vision, alone in the sweep of some prophetic intuition of mission immense in its finally mysterious reach of feeling and understanding, which not only the irritations of the Kennedys, but such indignations as he was hearing this evening all only partially, fractionally apprehended. Which was perhaps not even yet fully clear to King himself. But it was a sensed vastness of theme and plot that nevertheless had to encompass in it somehow even these angers around him now. And unlike his gracelessly blurting defensiveness when asked to join in the Freedom Rides, throughout this night's barrage of excoriation he was, to some bystanders, almost heartbreakingly apologetic, deferential, conciliatory, acceding that the movement's more impatiently aggressive young militants were serving as "the creative antagonists who constantly push us into positions where we should go further." Such acknowledgments were to prove increasingly insufficient to assuage the resentments already gathering toward the open belaborment that would beset King's last years. But at the end of this late-night backyard session in Albany, at least, many in the SNCC group had been unexpectedly touched by King's self-effacing and tormented earnestness.

Then that Friday, while King was kneeling with others in front of Albany's city hall, as if by way of some penance after the rebukes of five nights ago, he was arrested yet again. But not even this gesture of, in effect, throwing himself into jail for the third time was enough by now to rouse the weary, disappointed Albany Movement. King's sentence was suspended, and he was released — but it was into the dull emptiness of the campaign's virtual exhaustion.

The only promise of any last rescue had always been some intervention by the Justice Department. But Robert Kennedy, meeting in Washington with a delegation of other civil rights figures, had mentioned to them, for obvious wider circulation, that it would almost certainly take the removal of King's provocative presence from Albany before the city's government would negotiate with black leaders there. To that, the city replied with dispatch that it was agreeable to talks with any local "responsible, law-abiding" blacks — which of course excluded, as was shortly clarified, anyone arrested during demonstrations, meaning thereby almost all who had participated in the Albany Movement. Nevertheless, with Kennedy's pointed suggestion and the city's public response, King, desperate by this point for the most decorous exit possible out of Albany, offered once again, despite the experience the last time he made much the same proposal, that he would be "happy to leave . . . if I stand in the way of any negotiations which would be held in good faith." With King thus more or less serving notice that he was withdrawing from the field, the city commission advised local movement leaders that it could not enter into any considerations of their complaints until litigation under way in the courts was adjudicated. And with that, the same black leadership that had invited King into Albany some eight months before proclaimed an end to demonstrations and any hopes for negotiating with the present city authorities, declaring a shift instead to voter registration efforts to replace them.

So did King's Albany venture vapor out to its finish.

★ ★ ★

Commentary afterward in the national press was scorching, pointing out that, for all King's long exertions in Albany, "not a single racial barrier" had fallen, that the city remained "just as segregated as ever." More than that, the city library was now closed, as were the city parks, simply to avoid any blacks' seeking entrance to them. Claims of another sort of victory were bravely put forward anyway: that the number of blacks registered to vote had in fact more than doubled in Albany since the demonstrations, and more impalpable but perhaps more important, that simply in the experience of protest and confrontation, Albany's black community had liberated itself into a pride and unafraid sense of self it had never known before — that the Albany Movement had acted to remake the psyche of black citizens there.

That did turn out over time to be, beyond legislation and systemic reforms, the spiritual gift of the movement to blacks all over the South. But in Albany, King would plainly admit afterward, "I failed to do what I had hoped to do." Captive in a way of the symbol he had become, while also obsessed with keeping that symbol alive somehow, he'd been pulled into a conflict beyond his immediate initiation and direction. But allowing himself to be drawn into the insular complications of a largely preset situation was a mistake King realized he could never make again. From now on, he must carefully select and develop himself the setting and circumstances of any major commitment.

His disastrous misfire in Albany, though, had only accelerated the growing disdain for King among the fire-breathing young bravos in SNCC. Regulars in this group, now commonly called "Snick," began referring to King's SCLC as "Slick," and in Albany there had already begun to be heard the hoots that would haunt King in later years, "De Lawd! De Lawd!" as if he were some cartoon player strolled out of *The Green Pastures*. One in SNCC's ranks then, a thin and boyish Julian Bond, would briskly dismiss King as "a very simple man" who yet had somehow "sold the concept that one man will come to your town and save you." But "[he] has been losing since he left Montgomery. He lost when he didn't go on the Freedom Rides when the students begged him to. . . . He has been losing for a long time. And I think eventually that more Negroes and more white Americans will become disillusioned with him, and find that he after all is only another preacher who can talk well."

The fact is, King was always to fail more often than he would succeed. But throughout his confoundments since Montgomery, including now Albany, he yet remarkably seemed to keep growing — as if only magnified by his defeats — as, to the great masses of black Americans in those barren segregationist times, still the single most auspicious and moving figure of protest and hope, whether availing or not. Even so, Albany's most alarming implication for King was its peril as a precedent. Deprived by Pritchett's cunning of those convulsive clashes that would have dramatized for the rest of the country the underlying barbarity of its segregationist order, few in that larger national community, and certainly not the Kennedy administration, could be stirred to intercede. Such confrontations became then little more than tempests in a vacuum. And in that way, Albany had demonstrated, could King almost certainly always be defeated.

It was the conclusion of *Time* that King's frenetic efforts over the past five years had "drained him of the captivating fervor that made him famous." If not quite that, after his long ordeal of passionate but finally gainless oratory through that time, he had now discovered the limits as well as the euphoria of mass meetings, none of which could be more rousingly alive than those in Albany. More significant, though, he had also discovered in that dubious battle the limits of laboring to appeal to the larger conscience of whites. In short, the romance of Montgomery had at last come to its end in Albany; King realized now there were in fact to be no more Montgomerys. His predicament, though, was that even more critically did he need some authentic and momentous victory to keep alive the mission that Montgomery had thrown him into.

And there now arose for King a call promising a deliverance at last out of his past years of wandering in a wilderness of distraction and unconnection — a call to come to Birmingham.

Apotheosis

Spread along the last slopes of the Appalachian Mountains about a hundred miles above Montgomery, Birmingham was an Alabama outpost of the steel industry of the North, a burly, gritty, smokily sunlit city that liked to advertise itself as "the Pittsburgh of the South." Its affairs were mainly managed by a small proprietary circle called the Big Mules, along with an equally insular society known as the Senior Citizens, but they had allowed the city's rougher political prospectors to make Birmingham, with its population 40 percent black, one of the most formidable redoubts of segregation in all Dixie. That situation had been regularly reinforced by its sizable Klan contingent, with periodic cross burnings, occasional abductions and mutilations of blacks, and dynamite bombings of black churches and homes so commonplace that "the Pittsburgh of the South" was far more often referred to as "Bombingham."

A recipient of one of those bombings had been the parsonage of Fred Shuttlesworth, the obstreperous King aide and local preacher who had long been battling Birmingham's Brobdingnagian apartheid system and, for the past several years, clamoring for King to launch a concerted SCLC effort there. Already, actually, the SCLC had become marginally involved in Birmingham, and a series of student demonstrations in 1962 promoting a boycott of segregated downtown stores had begun drawing in more of its black citizenry, producing a substantial decline in sales, until the city commission had peremptorily intervened to forbid any concessions from the mercantile community.

But once King had announced a decision to move into Birmingham with a "full-scale assault," beginning in the spring of 1963, he became noticeably moody, indrawn, abstracted. Over the course of his bootless exercises since Montgomery, he had acquired the rather stale persona of a memento left over from the fifties, and after his inglorious withdrawal from Albany eight months before, if he did not prevail in the even more staggering task of truly transforming Birmingham, it was almost certainly all over with him as a figure of any relevance in the sixties. The enterprise there would have to be radically revised in approach. To begin with, King had recognized after Albany that he must take fully in hand himself a campaign for which the media, and therefore public belief, would hold him accountable anyway. Accordingly, Wyatt T. Walker plotted out a phased escalation of demonstrations to support a total boycott by Birmingham's blacks of the city's downtown commercial district — all to force a desegregation of the stores there, in both customer facilities and staff employed; a desegregation of movie theaters and motels; hiring equality for blacks in the city's government services, including policemen; a dropping of charges against all those arrested in earlier protests; and the formation of a biracial council to develop further civil rights initiatives. It was an agenda not that dissimilar in expansiveness from that in Albany, actually — but the difference was that, instead of being directed at the political authorities, who were free of any dependence on a black vote, the campaign would sight on the business community, which was most crucially dependent on black consumers, and should subsequently exert its considerable suasions on municipal and county officials.

Albany had also brought King to a harder reality: Birmingham must be an exertion of sheer massed popular power aside from merely moral expectations of its effect on the conscience of whites. Montgomery was indeed gone, in more ways than one. As Wyatt T. Walker posed it, "To make a moderate approach, hoping to get help from whites, doesn't work. They nail you to the cross." Only by an unrelentingly militant offensive to "surface tensions" in this particularly baleful citadel of segregation in the South — so forcing an open paroxysm of crisis that would bring the necessary notice of the media — would the Kennedy administration be obliged to act as they were able to evade doing in Albany, and press a resolution on Birmingham's government if its businessmen could not.

Perhaps the most inspiriting consideration in all this was that, in Birmingham, they would be facing not the guiles of a Laurie Pritchett, but the city's public safety commissioner for twenty-three years, Eugene "Bull" Connor, a bombastic segregationist of the old, unapologetically bluff sort — a podgy, strutful, middle-aged bossman in a snap-brim straw hat who knew only one word for King and his people, "nigger," and held a famously irascible temper. He was the factor the SCLC was counting on, "had calculated for," Wyatt T. Walker would later report.

As it happened, Connor had just been defeated in a race for mayor by a relatively temperate-toned segregationist, Albert Boutwell, supported by those civic interests sensitive to presenting a measure more respectability in conducting the city through its gathering racial duress. But Connor refused to relinquish his rule over the city's police and firemen, while challenging in the courts the legitimacy of Boutwell's election under the new city charter approved at the same time. All this had created a muddlement of, in effect, two contending governments in the city. Boutwell's election, too, had introduced into the situation the treacherous distraction of a prospect for new moderation in Birmingham's racial politics if he should take office, and until the courts finally decided between him and Connor, the city's business estate was paralyzed about entering into any consideration of black demands. For that matter, Robert Kennedy himself had termed any demonstrations "ill-timed," and the national press dismissed King's Birmingham venture with the customary cynicisms, *The Washington Post* discounting it as of "dubious utility," inspired more by King's ambitions "than by the real need of the situation." This was chilling for King's hopes of an indispensably important media witness in this decisive confrontation he had given himself over to. As Andrew Young would later attest, "The movement was really about getting publicity for injustice. . . . As long as it stayed below the surface, nobody was concerned about it. You had to bring it out into the open." But the perspective the press tended to share with not only the Kennedy administration but Birmingham's own comparatively progressive civic gentry was that both King and Connor were merely opposite but equally objectionable extremist provocateurs.

In fact, among Birmingham's black leadership itself, there was a reluctance about the "full scale" demonstrations King was vowing to mount, some fearing only a period of upheaval that would come to the same sort of blank end as Albany — this ambivalence among the black community's stewards necessitating urgent personal exhortations to them by King. Afterward, their most prestigious figure, wealthy business entrepreneur A. G. Gaston, agreed to King's settling with Abernathy in the master suite of his motel, right above its lobby, for their operating headquarters — just across Kelly Ingram Park from the Sixteenth Street Baptist Church, which was to turn into the central setting for the collisions to come.

★ ★ ★

Mass meetings commenced in Birmingham's black churches like a regular nightly rolling of kettledrums. Daddy King even appeared at one, having long since disposed of his reservations about his son's extra-ecclesiastical social calling, to resoundingly appeal to everyone to commit their bodies to the campaign (which, however, still did not quite include his son, as he would shortly make evident). King himself, striving to make his rhetoric count again after the limbo of the past six years, declaimed at church rallies, "Now, we say in this nonviolent movement that you've got to love this white man. And God knows, he needs our love," going on to expound again for these congregations the concept of agape: "And when you rise to love on *this* level . . . you love those that you don't like, you love those whose ways are distasteful to you. You love *every* man — because *God* loves him!" In a dialogue then playing back and forth between him and the congregation, as reported by biographer David Lewis, King would shout, "If the road to freedom leads through the jailhouse, then, turnkey, swing wide the gates!" *Preach, doctor, preach!* "Some of you are afraid." *That's right, that's right.* "Some of you are contented." *Speak, speak!* "But if you don't go, don't hinder me. We shall march nonviolently. We shall force this nation, this city, this world, to face its own conscience. We will make the God of love in the white man triumphant over the Satan of segregation that is in him. The struggle is not between black and white —" *No, no!* "But between good and evil!" *That's it, that's it!* "And whenever good and evil have a confrontation, good will win!"

There did occur one moment during the later stage of demonstrations, after Bull Connor had unlimbered his fire hoses, when King's old hope of moral appeal to the conscience of one's abusers seemed to breathe briefly into reality. A congregation broke out of a church on an impromptu march toward the city jail that was shortly stopped by a cordon of Bull Connor's police, water hoses held at the ready. Connor squalled out an order to turn on the hoses, but for some reason his men did not move, seemingly stricken motionless by the sight of these black churchfolk before them in their Sunday clothes. Connor bayed again, "Dammit, *turn on those hoses!*" But still, amazingly, his men did nothing. And Connor himself finally allowed the marchers to move past the poised fire hoses, through his ranked police, with cries of "Hallelujah" rippling back through the column, to hold a prayer service in a park a block beyond.

But Birmingham turned out a struggle for the most part far less transcendental than that. In fact, for all of King's oratorical steams, the campaign began only sputteringly, with nowhere near the anticipated number of demonstrators volunteering, and those meeting with a mystifying civility at first from Bull Connor in presiding over their arrests. Actually, Alabama's governor now, George Wallace — a stumpy, churningly combative segregationist and hotly glandular folk demagogue, who was shortly to become King's elemental antagonist — had earlier entered into a compact with Connor to dispatch state troopers into Birmingham to swiftly trample down demonstrations. They were deterred from this, however, by Boutwell's supporters in the city's management community, who, having conferred with Albany's Laurie Pritchett, insisted instead on his "velvet fist" sort of restrained resistance. King thus found Albany's strategy deployed against him once again, and after the first eight days of demonstrations, his crusade in the city seemed seriously stalled, with only some 150 protesters in jail so far, half the number arrested on just the first day of King's movement in Albany. To the national press, it was as if the whole affair were merely another negligible commotion in the succession of King's alarums and flash-outs. The entire undertaking was fast approaching the unthinkable: that Birmingham would wind up Albany all over again, and worse, without even reaching the size of that effort.

But Connor, not content with that likelihood, gave the first indication that his gangbuster disposition might yet be relied on when he additionally thought to pursue the Albany ploy of obtaining a court injunction against any further demonstrations — only it was not from a federal but from a congenial state judge. Which thereby gave King the opening to defy it without compromising the movement's concordat with federal authority. King had concluded by now it would take nothing less than his own imprisonment, by violating the injunction, to shock to life the flagging Birmingham campaign and pull into it the masses of black citizens still holding back, while at the same time electrifying the full attention of the media and the administration.

Even so, there weighed heavy logistical

concerns about King's being confined in Birmingham's jail at the moment: it would preclude his conducting a scheduled fund-raising tour critical for the campaign's bail resources for demonstrators. In a long morning session in the suite at the Gaston Motel with some two dozen advisers — including Daddy King, who, never gladdened by the prospect of his son in jail, insisted he forgo defying the injunction — King travailed over the conflict of imperatives. If, by leaving to try salvaging the movement from its financial emergency, it appeared he was complying with the injunction by not marching and being arrested, as he had already publicly announced he would, "we are out of business" anyway, he submitted. Finally, over the din of argument in the suite, he declared he needed to pray on the matter and went into his bedroom and shut the door. About thirty minutes later, the furor of discussion still under way in the sitting room was abruptly hushed when he came back out the bedroom door, clad now in a workshirt and stiff new denim jeans, their cuffs rolled up over new brogans. "I don't know where the money will come from, but I have to make a faith act," he announced. "I've got so many people depending on me, I've got to march."

That afternoon — which happened to be Good Friday — King and Abernathy set out from a mass meeting at Sixteenth Street Church, across the park from the motel, on a march headed toward city hall, accompanied only by some forty other marchers. They had proceeded just a few blocks when they encountered a barricade of Connor's men, one of whom — in a momentary lapse from their protocol of courtesy, with King himself now in hand — snatched him by the back of his belt, hitching him off his feet and heaving him into the back of a paddy wagon. Carried to Birmingham's jail then, King was pitched alone into the gloom of a narrow, windowless cell, with a cot of only metal slats, bare of mattress. He was denied contact with anyone, whether by visit or phone call, over the next two days — their passage marked only by faint blurrings and wanings of light over his cell door — on into Easter afternoon. He would later relate, "You will never know the meaning of utter darkness until you have lain in such a dungeon," and "there was more to the blackness than a phenomenon conjured up by a worried mind. . . ."

Among the newspapers slipped in for King to read under the wan glare of the cell's light bulb was a copy of the *Bir-*

mingham News with a story headlined WHITE CLERGYMEN URGE LOCAL NEGROES TO WITHDRAW FROM DEMONSTRATIONS. In a joint statement, eight local clerical dignitaries, who, though their own congregations were segregated, had earlier voiced commendably liberal racial sentiments, now reproved King and his "outsiders" for their "extremism" in provoking "unwise and untimely" civil disturbances inciting "hatred and violence," which "have not contributed to the resolution of our local problems," maintaining that instead all appeals for redress by the city's subject black population "should be pressed in the courts, and in negotiations among local leaders, not in the streets." Earlier, in Albany, to a curiously similar complaint from the NAACP — not that distant from the Kennedys' own sensibilities, actually — King had replied that "legislation and court orders can only declare rights. They can never thoroughly deliver them. Only when the people themselves begin to act are rights on paper given life blood." That difference — between rights by law and rights actualized on the ground — was always to be one of King's central conflicts with the system around him.

And now, something about this rebuke

from fellow ministers in Birmingham, eminently decent men all, urging patience out of the same preoccupation with a seemly moderation of which King himself had been accused by the SNCC activists in Albany — something about their reproach seemed to instantly obsess King. He began scrawling a reply to their statement on the margins of the newspaper until he had filled every available cranny of its pages with dense scribblings, connective arrows and circlings. When an aide was finally admitted for a visit to discuss the campaign's legal and financial extremities, King simply withdrew the newspaper from under his shirt, saying, "I'm writing this letter. I want you to try to get it out," and then took several sheets from the aide's notepad: "I'm not finished yet. . . ." He went on writing over the next three days, shuffling the pages between the bars to the aide, black attorney Clarence Jones, whenever he reappeared. Jones began to fear King had lost his hold on the reality of things outside the jail, but King only told him, "I need more paper."

It turned out, when typed, to be a twenty-page disquisition — and proved one occasion in which his writing matched his pulpit voltages, coming as it did from thinking in action in the immediate heat of a crisis.

King's "Letter from Birmingham Jail" constituted, really, his comprehensive reply at last to all the accumulated cautionings and skepticisms up to now, from parties like the Kennedys to these excellent reverends in Birmingham, about the legitimacy of his confrontational movement apostleship — an exegesis that came close, as his own personal manifesto, to that profession of faith hammered to the door of Wittenberg's Castle Church by his namesake four hundred years before.

"Frankly," King pointed out for his pastoral colleagues, "I have yet to engage in a direct action campaign that was 'well-timed' in the view of those who have not suffered unduly from the disease of segregation." He detailed for them in a long symphonic chronicling how blacks had already endured more than three centuries of dehumanization and abasement in America, and averred that "it is easy for those who have never felt the stinging darts of segregation to say, 'Wait.'" But "when you are harried by day and haunted by night by the fact that you are a Negro, living constantly at a tip-toe stance, never quite knowing what to expect next, and plagued with inner fears and outer resentments, when you are forever fighting a degenerating sense of 'nobodiness'; then you will understand why we find it difficult to wait." And if they supposed they were themselves isolated and exempt in their pleasant white world from the abuses visited on their fellow black citizens, he warned, "Injustice anywhere is a threat to justice everywhere."

Expressing an astonished dismay that they had commended the good behavior of the police in containing the demonstrations, he asserted that it was a fundamental corruption to approve "moral means to preserve immoral ends." He only wished, he submitted, that they had also "commended the Negro sit-inners and demonstrators of Birmingham for their sublime courage, their willingness to suffer. . . ." The truth was, he proposed, it would be the protesting demonstrators in the South who would someday be recognized as the "real heroes" of these times, "carrying our whole nation back to those great wells of democracy which were dug deep by the founding fathers." King went on to lament, "I have almost reached the regrettable conclusion that the Negro's greatest stumbling block is not the White Citizens Council-er or the Ku Klux Klanner, but the white moderate who is more devoted to 'order' than to justice." Indeed, he declared to these religious worthies of Birmingham: "Shallow under-standing from people of good will is more frustrating than absolute understanding from people of ill will."

It was that shallow understanding that produced objections like theirs about extremist actions, King asserted. But the "question is not whether we will be extremists, but what kind of extremists we will be." King proceeded then to celebrate, for the ministers' edification, such extremists as the prophet Amos, Jesus, Jefferson, Lincoln. (In this, King could not know he was venturing bizarrely close to the famous proclamation about eighteen months later of the dread Barry Goldwater on his nomination as the Republican presidential candidate: "Extremism in the defense of liberty is no vice....")

But before he was done, King's meditations to the ministers had ranged out beyond his own circumstances in Birmingham's jail, beyond even the South in the sixties, out into the whole movement of history, casting Birmingham in that ultimate perspective with citations from St. Paul, Socrates, Thomas Aquinas, T. S. Eliot, Martin Buber: with these invocations and applications from all his reading since Crozer and Boston University, King's exegesis from Birmingham's jail became, some eight years now after his formal academic one, his true doctoral thesis. "I would agree with St. Augustine that 'an unjust law is no law at all,' " he posited to his fellow ministers in Birmingham. But anyone "who breaks an unjust law must do it openly, lovingly," accepting imprisonment "to rouse the conscience of the community over its injustices," an act "in reality expressing the very highest respect for the law."

King's letter, when it reached the eight clergymen, drew not a single response. Rather, it was as if they'd found their remarks had brought an exegetical avalanche unloading down on them, and one of them, after reading through it, merely sighed to an assistant, "This is what you get when you try to do something. . . ." But Wyatt T. Walker, who had frenetically directed the typing of King's scrawlings as they were transmitted to him, was euphoric at being on hand for the creation of what he felt sure was another epistle like those of the early apostles in prison, and when it was completed, he distributed it widely about. Yet it would be a month before any mention of King's "Letter from Birmingham Jail" appeared anywhere in the press, and much longer before it would be recognized as King's great testament — profounder than his majestic oration at the Washington March a few months later.

As it turned out, though, King's jailing had stirred little of the anticipated effects outside: the Birmingham endeavor was still in imminent danger of ending up stillborn. And after nine days in his cell, King agreed to being released with a payment of his bail. But at a mass meeting that night — the twenty-fifth straight one so far — the crowd was still dismally small. Meanwhile, the vital oxygen of media coverage was rapidly thinning away altogether. "We've got to pick up everything, because the press is leaving," King fumed. "We've got to *get going.*" Indications had reached him that serious biracial deliberations with the city's merchants were prepared to commence, but he had learned from Albany the disaster of forestalling demonstrations on such airy prospects. Nevertheless, Wyatt T. Walker would recall, "We had run out of troops. We had scraped the bottom of the barrel of adults who could go."

Then James Bevel, who had been called in from fieldwork in Mississippi, again demonstrated his wizardlike genius, which had always fascinated King, for a flourish of

inspired wildness to deliver a situation out
of such a critical cul-de-sac: He had long
operated from the belief that the only
proper answer sometimes to the mad pa-
thologies of segregation was a certain corre-
sponding craziness. And he now hit upon
the idea of mobilizing Birmingham's high
school students to furnish demonstrations
of a properly impressive size. King was initially hesitant. "If all these kids are out of
school," he worried to a friend, Alabama's
state troopers "are going to beat them."
Later on, such a gambit would appall the
Kennedys as the most dubious sort of reck-
less and somehow tasteless recourse:
"School children participating in street
demonstrations is a dangerous business,"
Robert Kennedy would observe in bitten
tones. "An injured, maimed, or dead child
is a price that none of us can afford to pay."
Birmingham's own black leadership was itself at first aghast at the idea of subjecting
their children to the brutalizations of arrest
and jailing by Bull Connor's forces — and
were aware as well that anyone advocating
such a measure could themselves be prosecuted for contributing to the delinquency of
a minor.

But King was at a grim edge. There
seemed nothing else left. His decision in the

end to enlist Birmingham's schoolchildren in his sagging campaign was, for many years afterward, to discomfort a great number of otherwise admiring parties as a reach of brazen, if not craven, opportunism. But while King remained uneasy about employing such means, he soon sensed it was the kind of commitment to a final, rash, risky, extreme, and questionable act that more than once in history had wound up deciding everything for seemingly hopeless causes. His aides, too, insisted it was a "leap of faith," as Walker put it, that they must brave to save their Birmingham effort. In subsequent mass meetings, King would undertake to reassure the city's black community, and very likely himself as well, "Now, finally, your children, your daughters and sons, are in jail. . . . They are suffering for what they believe, and they are suffering to make this a better nation." They were, in fact, King declared, winning for themselves, with their own courage and endurance, their own freer future, an experience for which their elders should envy them.

In what became over the next seven days something like a 1963 Birmingham evocation of the Children's Crusade, hundreds of youngsters, in age from sixteen to as young as six, teemed clapping and singing out of

Sixteenth Street Church in successive waves, directed by James Bevel in his skullcap, sweeping on to Kelly Ingram Park, where Bull Connor's police were waiting to pack them all into paddy wagons — and, when those were unable to hold their numbers, into school buses — for transport to Birmingham's jail. On the very first day, five hundred were arrested. When Birmingham's jail facilities could no longer contain them, hundreds more were deposited in an outdoor stockpen at the fairgrounds. And with this sudden threat of simply being overrun by demonstrators, it was now that Bull Connor's dependably primitive reflexes at last brawled into the open.

He ordered swung on the young marchers high-pressure water hoses that battered them back, along with black onlookers, with a force that ripped the clothes off some; and then bawling, "I want to see the dogs work," set on them snarling German shepherds, Connor whooping happily, "Look at those niggers run!" One news photo of a policeman clutching the shirtfront of a black youth with one hand while his other held the leash of a dog swirling at the youth's midsection happened to pass under the eyes of the president in the Oval Office, and he told a group of visitors that day, "It makes me sick." But still the swells of young demonstrators kept coming, those arrested immediately replaced by yet more. Connor improvised a special superforce water cannon mounted on a tripod that could blast bark off trees a hundred feet away, this contrivance blowing marchers back like rag dolls, along with the black bystanders who'd begun collecting to toss rocks and bottles at Connor's men. Shuttlesworth himself was once slammed by the water cannon against a wall with such pile-driving impact, he had to be carried on a stretcher to an ambulance. Afterward, Connor expressed the wish that "they'd carried him away in a hearse."

With all this, Birmingham suddenly flared onto the nightly network newscasts and the front pages of newspapers across the nation — and the visions of Bull Connor's forces turning fire-hose bombardments and swarming police dogs on fleeing black youths were of a simple savagery a quantum leap beyond all reservations about the seemliness of using teenage demonstrators. And as a host of journalists came milling into the city, the symbiosis between the movement and the media came now into its full realization. Since Montgomery, television had been expanding like the slow-motion explosion of a new energy in the atmosphere in its capacity for massive collective witness, and now, when almost everything could be beheld by everyone almost at once, Birmingham became a crisis the whole country was experiencing. Among the black community in the city itself, this spectacle of the innate viciousness of Birmingham's racist order unleashed on their children served to erase any ambivalences left about King's campaign, consolidating behind it the black elite and common citizenry alike, many adults now joining their children in the marches. King's Birmingham movement had at last come surgingly alive: in the phrase of evangelists for a revival finally taking in a community, it had "broken through."

Up to now, Connor's police actions had managed to keep marches from spilling out of the black neighborhoods and actually reaching downtown Birmingham. But then, simultaneous forays by some fifteen separate detachments of demonstrators succeeded in outflanking his fire hoses and dogs and whirled into the downtown streets of the city, coursing jubilantly along the noontime sidewalks with a choiring of "We Shall Overcome" to the startled stares of white shoppers and businessmen on their lunch hour, who eyed this irruption out of the city's black precincts as if it were an incursion of Visigoths into the center of Rome. It was, however, altogether more celebration than raid, with no breakage or vandalism. But it left the center of the city in following days eerily blank, producing what amounted to a boycott by white shoppers as well.

Birmingham's business community now determined they must finally begin talks in earnest with the black leadership, "though the idea of negotiations," one of them sniffed, "was offensive to all of us." But if they did not, the dread was that the city would be locked into this blighting boycott by an occupation by George Wallace's state troopers or the Alabama National Guard. At the same time, remarkably, Robert Kennedy had begun to perceive by now, as he advised a delegation of Alabama newspaper editors, that "if King loses, worse leaders are going to take his place," suggesting they should count themselves fortunate he happened to be as moderate and nonviolent as he was. It was as if the images of outrage out of Birmingham had radically altered everything, including the understanding of the Kennedys. Robert Kennedy and his deputies began their own campaign of strenuous persuasion to facilitate the biracial discussions now under way in the city. With Andrew Young primarily negotiating for King in his calm and carefully measured manner, the deliberations continued on through one long night until, at four in the morning, the fundaments of a settlement were agreed to.

But the afternoon before, a riot had erupted in Kelly Ingram Park, a contagion of defiance now drawing a ruder crowd out of nearby bars and poolrooms to war with bricks and rocks against Connor's fire hoses. King thus decided, with the negotiations having reached the sensitive point of a likely settlement, to call a one-day moratorium on protests. This infuriated Shuttlesworth, just out of the hospital, who'd come to feel he'd already been shuffled aside over the course of the Birmingham campaign. "Well, Martin, it's hard for me to see how anybody could decide that without me," he blazed at King. "Ain't no use scalding the hog on one side. While the water's hot, scald 'im on both sides and get 'im clean!" He railed on, "You know they said in Albany that you come in, get people excited and started, and you leave town. But I live here, and I'm telling you, [demonstrations] will *not* be called off!" King was visibly distressed, murmurously propitiatory at this surprising outburst, but Shuttlesworth blared on, "You're in a hell of a fix, young man . . . You're Mister Big, but you're going to be Mister S-h-i-t!" It was a tirade that astonished the others gathered there in its raw and almost hysteric disrespect, but King merely took Shuttlesworth off into another room, where after minutes of talking to him alone, he managed to mollify him. At a subsequent press conference, then — over 170 reporters, including foreign press, had now mobbed into Birmingham — King allowed Shuttlesworth to make the announcement of the pending agreement, Shuttlesworth proudly proclaiming, "The city of Birmingham has reached an accord with its conscience. . . ." Whereupon, having arrived at this apparent victorious dawn to his years of raging against the long night of segregation in Birmingham, he collapsed in a faint.

But with word that an agreement was near on the demands of Birmingham's black citizens, Connor locked the doors of Sixteenth Street Church, and Wallace sent in his state troopers under the command of Colonel Al Lingo, their steel helmets painted with the Confederate flag, to conduct drill exercises in Kelly Ingram Park across from the church. Connor then had King's bail for his

Good Friday arrest raised to $2,500, knowing King would refuse to pay the increase, as a way to get him back in jail — all this to excite an upheaval that would wreck the pending settlement. Indications that King, arrested again, meant to stay in jail to prolong tensions in the city baffled Robert Kennedy as simply perverse, and he persuaded Gaston to bail him out. But King announced that if no settlement were concluded the next morning, demonstrations would resume, and on a larger scale than Birmingham had yet seen. Final agreement still hung on the terms for release of the other 2,500 arrested demonstrators, and Robert Kennedy himself now quietly scrambled to rummage up the necessary $160,000 in bail money, primarily from the nation's major labor unions. Shortly after this sum was rushed to Birmingham, the city's Big Mules and the Senior Citizens affirmed their arrangement with Young and A. G. Gaston on the other particulars. The fitting rooms of stores would be desegregated immediately and, in phases then, lunch counters and water fountains and rest rooms, black sales clerks employed, with a biracial committee to work out the other means for fully opening up to blacks at last the public life of Birmingham.

This, with only eight days having passed since the first student demonstrations — seven weeks since the beginning of King's Birmingham offensive.

But havoc followed. The night after the agreement's announcement, Birmingham's cityscape was lit by bomb glares, one blasting apart the front of the parsonage of King's younger brother, A.D. — who, with King's short, chunky look and the same bland, round face, had, through a succession of pastorates made shaky by his already apparent whiskey troubles, nevertheless been sedulously serving at the edges of his older brother's progress. A few moments after that explosion, another wrecked the lobby of the Gaston Motel, right under the suite, unoccupied at the time, from which King had been directing the Birmingham campaign. Shades of the future were held in the dark hours that followed. The bombings set off a roaring riot around Kelly Ingram Park, cars burned, stores set aflame, by that dispossessed and trapped underclass population of blacks who all along had little to hope for themselves from the terms of any negotiated settlement, and whose furies nationally enlarged before long were to come near devouring King's movement. This uproar in

Kelly Ingram Park, though, provided exactly the occasion for Wallace to set Al Lingo's state troopers finally storming into action, they clubbing their way through the riot in a rampage of their own that also prefigured, in the darkness of that night, the ferocity later at the Selma Bridge.

At the White House, the president's concern now, with Wallace having already vowed to personally block two black students from entering the University of Alabama, was that this surly little political gremlin had, as Kennedy remarked incredulously, "virtually taken over the state." Yet for all the bombings and turmoil and Wallace's storm trooper strikes — the agreement in Birmingham held. Incredibly, it held.

Six years after the Montgomery boycott had prevailed only through the last-moment judgment in the federal court suit, Birmingham had become the first clear, authentic victory, actually won in popular confrontation and struggle, for King's movement of nonviolent mass protest. As the campaign was nearing its climax, Stanley Levison had told King, "No question, if this comes, this is the big one." Birmingham became in fact King's true apotheosis. Only now had he at last realized the expectations that had settled on him in Montgomery, and it restored him in the national regard, with indisputable legitimacy this time, as the single most significant figure — indeed, in a realm really unto himself — of the American civil rights movement. After his Birmingham victory, King found himself, only some ten months after the press derision over his capsizing in Albany, now on the cover of *Time* as its 1963 "Man of the Year." King himself declared, in exultation at this reaffirmation of the epiphany that had come to him in his kitchen that midnight in Montgomery, "There are certain spiritual experiences that we continue to have" in which one "knows deep down within there is something in the very structure of the cosmos that will ultimately bring about fulfillment and the triumph of what is right. And this is the only thing that can keep one going in difficult periods."

More, Birmingham had set off the wider repercussions of other demonstrations — 758 of them by one tabulation, in 186 cities and towns reaching even beyond the South — for open access to public accommodations. The Kennedy administration now contemplated the possibility of an outbreak of multiple Birminghams across the entire country. Only some two and a half years since the Kennedys' initial efforts to consign King and his moralizings to the outskirts of pertinence, the civil rights revolution seemed about to overwhelm the Kennedy presidency: "It's just in everything," the president marveled at one point, "I mean, this has become everything." But both Kennedys had been shanghaied by events into a recognition, finally, of the nation's unavoidable moral covenant with history on the matter of its racial inequities. It brought the president to what he'd never reckoned on having to hazard during his first term — proposing a comprehensive civil rights bill on public accommodations, though he well knew it would most likely reconfigure party alignments in the South lasting since Reconstruction, turning that quarter of the country into a white Republican fastness.

On a brassily hot June day at the University of Alabama, Deputy Attorney General Nicholas Katzenbach instructed a stubby and sullen George Wallace that he must step aside from barring admission of two black students to the school. And that evening, President Kennedy appeared on national television to deliver one of his own most moving personal professions of conscience:

> We are confronted primarily with a moral issue. It is as old as the Scriptures and as clear as the American Constitution. If an American, because his skin is dark, cannot eat lunch in a restaurant open to the public, if he cannot send his children to the best public schools available . . . then who among us would be content to have the color of his skin changed? Who among us would then be content with counsels of patience and delay? . . .
> I am therefore asking the Congress to enact legislation giving all Americans the right to be served in facilities which are open to the public — hotels, restaurants, theaters, retail stores. . . .

The public accommodations bill would be the first of the two momentous pieces of civil rights legislation to be accomplished by King's movement in the South. But it was to be delivered into law by another president. Only some five months after John Kennedy's message that evening came the quick rifle cracks in the bright noon at Dallas. King, at home watching the first television reports with Coretta, murmured, "This is what is going to happen to me. . . ."

He lay sick in bed through the next two days of the nation's communal mourning through television's black-and-gray wake. Then — though not invited to Kennedy's funeral mass, as he had not been invited to his inauguration — King pulled himself out of bed to travel, totally alone, to Washington, where he stood by himself along a street for the funeral procession from the church to Arlington Cemetery.

II

The summer before that November noon in Dallas, on a hotly shining August day in the familiar postcard setting of the Washington Mall, with the monumental seated figure of Lincoln gazing down, as it were, on his still-ramifying consequences, an enormous multitude gathered over the grassy spaces below him — some quarter-million people, almost a third of them white, stretching back to the Washington Monument, a panoramic host of the movement's black faithful, white union regulars with placards, figures from America's pop galaxy of celebrity, simple believers who had journeyed there from communities across the country. Coming three months after King's Birmingham triumph, the March on Washington was like the annunciation of the civil rights movement's arrival as the nation's high decency, and King as its preeminent figure.

This mass pilgrimage into Washington had been entrepreneured by movement patriarch A. Philip Randolph, in concert with other leaders like King and, despite his crankiness about the SCLC's ascendancy after Birmingham, Roy Wilkins, to demonstrate the expanse and spirit of the movement with a colossal rally to appeal to Congress for passage of the public accommodations bill presented by Kennedy. The president himself, however, was more than a little edgy about it all, trying to dissuade the march's organizers with warnings, in a conversation with them beforehand, that thousands of demonstrators converging into the capital could be seen by Congress as an attempt at mob intimidation, resulting in their all losing the legislation he'd introduced, many on the Hill already looking for a pretext anyway to avoid supporting it. King offered the observation he had put to Birmingham's ministers: "Frankly, I have never engaged in any direct-action movement which did not seem ill-timed. Some people thought Birmingham ill-timed." To which the president rejoined, with a small smile, "Including the Attorney General."

In fact, there was a similar distress among the event's leadership about the hair-raisingly provocative tone of a speech that SNCC chairman John Lewis meant to deliver that day, mimeographed copies already being circulated about. "The revolution is at hand," it partly read. "We will take matters into our hands. . . . We will march through the South, through the heart of Dixie, the way Sherman did. We shall pursue our own 'scorched earth' policy and burn Jim Crow to the ground, nonviolently." The White House was scandalized when they read a copy of the speech, and the Catholic prelate of Washington served notice he would refuse to deliver the invocation if it were not amended. Actually, though he was a survivor by now of twenty-two arrests and a dozen beatings, it seemed improbably ferocious language to be coming from the gentle soul of Lewis, and only moments before he was to speak, in a feverish session in a small room right behind Lincoln's titanic effigy, King and several other march leaders labored to persuade him to revise the speech's more apocalyptic passages, King telling him, in that quiet, mild, rueful manner that his aides had always found almost impossible to resist, "John, I think I know you well. I don't think this sounds like you." Indeed, those flammable passages had, as it turned out, been pressed on Lewis by SNCC's more revolutionary provocateurs. And he revised the lines at the last second, on a portable typewriter behind Lincoln's statue.

Then, as the day wore on — with spirited addresses from Randolph, Lewis, Roy Wilkins, songs from Joan Baez, Marian Anderson, Bob Dylan, Mahalia Jackson — it all turned into a kind of massive worship service of rejoicing purpose. King's turn to speak came at the end of the program, and it wasn't until he had begun moving into his written text that he felt an impulse, "just all of a sudden, I don't know why, I hadn't thought about it before," to shift instead into the motif of a speech he'd already delivered more than once before, most recently in Detroit and Chicago. With an awkwardly straining gear change at first, he began, "I say to you today, my friends, so even though we face the difficulties of today and tomorrow — I still have a dream. . . ."

He brought now for the first time, to millions across the nation watching the live telecast on all three networks, those pulpit grandeurs of the revival services of his origins, the oratorical raptures of countless mass meetings in black sanctuaries over the South:

> . . . I have a dream that one day on the red hills of Georgia, the sons of former slaves and the sons of former slave-owners will be able to sit down together at the table of brotherhood. I have a dream —

It had suddenly become a pentecostal moment. A huge shiver of exhilaration moved through the expanses of the throng, shouts, bursts of clapping.

> I have a dream that my four little children will one day live in a nation where they will not be judged by the color of their skin but the content of their character. I have *a dream* today!

A running surf of cries and applause was now gathering after the baritone amplitudes of his voice:

> So let freedom ring! . . . Let freedom ring

from Stone Mountain of Georgia. Let freedom ring from every hill and molehill of Mississippi, from every mountainside. And when *this* happens — when we allow freedom to ring from every town and every hamlet, from every state and every city, we will be able to speed up that day when *all* God's children — black men and white men, Jews and Gentiles, Protestants and Catholics — will be able to join hands and sing in the words of the old Negro spiritual, *Free at last, free at last, thank God Almighty, we are free at last!*

And he swung away from the lectern, swamped with sweat. There was a hush — then a mammoth ovation in which, as it rolled through the multitude massed over Washington Mall, Coretta, watching from nearby, would remember that "the Kingdom of God seemed to have come on earth."

Watching on television at the White House, President Kennedy muttered, "He's damned good. Damned good." A short while after the rally's conclusion, when the march's organizers came by for a visit, Kennedy shook King's hand and told him, with a taut little nod of tribute, "*I* have a dream."

For King, the whole occasion — with its vision, if only for those few hours on Washington Mall, of a possible American Blessed Community — quickened his excitement that his nonviolent movement held the power to actually redeem the soul of the whole nation.

It did seem during those summer days of 1963 that the movement had gained a heady reach of promise — but it was a promise still shadowed by predatory and bloody menace. The very night that Kennedy had made his "moral issue" television address announcing he would be introducing a public accommodations bill to Congress, down in Jackson, Mississippi, the NAACP's state field secretary, Medgar Evers, returning home late from a strategy meeting, was shot to death in his driveway by a white supremacist, Byron De La Beckwith, who'd been waiting for him in the dark in a honeysuckle thicket across the street. Then, only a little over two weeks after the Washington March, on a Sunday morning in Birmingham, reprisal for the city's civil rights accord the past spring was exacted with a bomb explosion demolishing much of Sixteenth Street Church from which so many marches had sallied forth. In the wreckage were found the bodies of four young black girls, all in white Sunday dresses. The disorder that quickly spread over the city, in which two more black youths were slain, portended a race war about to erupt, and Wallace promptly sent in Al Lingo's storm troopers again, while managing to suggest that the bombing was likely the handiwork of black agitators to create sympathy for their cause.

Cast so quickly from the splendor of possibilities at the Washington March to this hellish reassertion of the lower, bestial realities still persisting, King seemed at first stunned into a strange sort of stupor. He did rouse himself, though, to journey to Birmingham to conduct the funeral for three of the girls, attended by the largest interracial assembly of ministers, coming from over the nation, that the city had ever seen, though none of the local pastors to whom he had addressed his jail letter were reported to be among them. Yet King struggled to preach, over the three caskets, his nonviolent message still: "History has proven over and over again that unmerited suffering is redemptive. . . . The innocent blood of these little girls may well serve as the redemptive force that will bring new light to this dark city." And he went on to insist, almost grotesquely now as it struck some there, "We must not lose faith in our white brothers. Somehow we must believe that the most misguided among them can learn to respect the dignity and worth of all human personality."

Nevertheless, King was unable to contain the rage even within the SCLC over the bombing. James Bevel's wife, Diane Nash, proposed nothing less than an all-out siege of the state of Alabama — actually surrounding the capital in Montgomery to cut it off from contact with the outside world, demonstrators lying on rail tracks and airport runways to halt transport in and out of the city, congesting its telephone lines, closing down its power company, along with a general work stoppage and refusal to pay taxes — all to force the removal of Wallace from office, declaring his government "null and void," while launching a crusade over all Alabama to register to vote every black citizen over the age of twenty. When Diane Nash presented this blitzkrieg prospectus to King, he chuckled uncomfortably and said, "Oh, Diane, now, wait, wait, now. Let's think about this. . . ." But it met with enthusiasm from other SCLC staffers as a way at least to actively answer the monstrousness of the church bombing, and would eventually evolve into the more muted form of a statewide voter registration project. In preparation for that, the SCLC soon extended its operations into the drowsing little black-belt city of Selma.

King, though, had not failed to sense a sullen sea change settling into the movement, conceding once that "the Negro in the South can now be nonviolent as a stratagem, but he can't include loving the white man." Well before the contretemps over Lewis's speech at the Washington March, in fact, King had come to feel caught up in a race against a deterioration in the moral terms of the movement, with the angry stridors of fire breathers like SNCC's Stokely Carmichael and James Forman, who had never been able to forgive finding King, while demonstrators were clashing with Bull Connor's police in Birmingham, eating a steak lunch in his pajamas in his suite at the Gaston Motel. King was confiding concerns now about how, with the black masses increasingly freed from old fears, "we will keep this fearlessness from rising to violent proportions," with "more and more bitterness because things haven't moved fast enough." Outside a church in Harlem, he had even been jeered, eggs flung at him, and afterward he ruminated somewhat lugubriously to Robert Penn Warren in an interview about "moments when you think about . . . the sacrifices and suffering you face, that your own people don't have an understanding, not even an appreciation, and seeking to destroy your image at every point." But he was repeatedly confronted with questions from the press as to whether the mood in the black community was not turning against his nonviolent gospel.

Out of the rancors that seemed to be radiating through black America appeared a tall, lanky figure even seen louring at the edges of the Washington March — Malcolm X. A onetime Harlem street hustler turned austere evangelist for the Islamic racial subsect known as the Black Muslims, Malcolm had come to parallel King's progress like some phantom figure of wrath, the shade of Nat Turner or Denmark Vesey returned out of the wilder reaches of the black past in America. His gangly, slat-thin, funereal-suited frame, hatted and bespectacled, towering over street rallies of inner-city blacks — a flat, cold glare in his eyes, spearing his forefinger in the air — he excoriated the white race in level, deliberate, quick licks of scorn: "We don't want to have anything to do with any race of dogs. Two-legged white dogs siccing four-legged dogs on your and my mother!"

In a sense, King and Malcolm were to pose the two potentials held within the turbulent Black Awakening of the sixties, the two temperaments contending for the future of black America. If, as some had already averred, King's vision of a nonviolent struggle of moral confrontation that would regenerate an essentially racist and barbarous society supposed too much of the human species, then Malcolm's seemed a vision of humankind's nature reduced to the most base and elementary terms of rage and retribution for abuse. Only fools "could love someone who has treated them as the white man has treated you," he proclaimed to his black audiences, styling their tormentor a "blue-eyed white devil" genetically beyond any moral appeal, really only a "bleached" parody of a human being, "an ole pale sickly-looking thing," but a predator nonetheless who could be handled only with threat and force. In truth, it was a racial invective that was merely an inverse of what could be heard at any cow-pasture Klan rally of that time. But Malcolm had become one of those black figures who periodically rise up before the shocked gaze of white society as a kind of demoniac reflection of its own systematic dehumanizations, at once a casualty of and judgment upon America's racism, its own tortured creature — as great crimes have immemorially had a way of imprinting themselves on their victims, they assuming something of the same nature of the violations worked upon them as one defense against those violations being performed upon them again. The racial malevolence of Malcolm's message, as King himself once observed, was "not so much an indictment against him as it is against a society whose ills in race relations are so deep-rooted that it produces a Malcolm X."

They were, King and Malcolm, really projections of two entirely different cultures. King's was a ministry congenial to his mostly churchly, respectably middle-class black constituency, eager to join in a coalition of purpose with the nation's white liberal establishment. But Malcolm was a prophet to another America, having arisen out of a childhood of cold misery that could not have been more unlike King's snugly privileged upbringing, and the vicious and gaudy hustler society of the black underclass in those mammoth ghettos of the North's "great cities of destruction," in E. Franklin Frazier's phrase. Such inner exiles lived without any sense of connection to the rest of the country, bereft of that sense of their individual worth without which "they cannot live," as James Baldwin wrote during the time, and "they will do anything whatever to regain it. That is why the most dangerous creation of any society is that man who has nothing to lose."

While Malcolm's fulminations seemed to whites to carry an unappeasable malignance, a radioactive field of menace, he also bestowed a sulfurous disdain on the civil rights movement and its leaders, for what he regarded as a craven appeal for integration out of some perverse urge of the abused "to unite" with their abusers. All the movement was achieving for black people anyway was "promises that they will be able to sit down and drink some coffee with some crackers in a cracker restaurant." He particularly despised the principle of nonviolence: "I believe it's a crime for anyone who is being brutalized to continue to accept that brutality without doing something to defend himself. . . . You might see these Negroes who believe in nonviolence and mistake us for one of them and put your hands on us thinking that we're going to turn the other cheek — and we'll put you to death just like *that!*" For King himself he reserved a special contempt, pronouncing him a "traitor to the Negro people."

King, for his part, deplored Malcolm's

"demagogic oratory," declaring that his "litany of articulating the despair of the Negro without offering any positive, creative alternative" had only "done himself and our people a great disservice." It was as if they were talking, living in, two totally different languages. They did encounter each other once, but that only glancingly, when both happened to be in the corridors of the Capitol during the debate on the 1964 public accommodations bill. Malcolm, spying King, swiftly leapt to his side, and they exchanged pleasantries and briefly clasped hands in a stammer of flashbulbs, King's smile a bit faint and tentative, but Malcolm with a spacious grin. They quickly parted then, and returned to their separate destinies. But King was to be increasingly haunted now by Malcolm's specter.

All this while, J. Edgar Hoover had continued his implacable covert pursuit of King, who, still refusing to disconnect from Stanley Levison, had become for Hoover a manifestation of interracial Communist sexual depravity all in one. When *Time* named King its "Man of the Year" after Birmingham, Hoover snorted in a remark passed around the Bureau, "They had to dig deep in the garbage for this one." King, as usual during times when he felt adversities closing in on him, was still retreating into carnal binges, these abandons to the flesh diligently taped by the FBI; and when Hoover was presented one "highlight" reel with an eight-page synopsis, it brought from him the exclamation, "This will destroy the burr-head!" As late as the eighties, FBI operatives were to claim to Taylor Branch that, though they themselves had not heard them, tapes of King's hotel room assignations had him shouting, "I'm fucking for God." Other reported outbursts — including an alleged comment while watching a rerun of television funeral footage of Jacqueline Kennedy kneeling beside the slain president's casket (an account of which Hoover quickly relayed to still–Attorney General Robert Kennedy) — were of a gross obscenity that, if true, would have indicated a kind of madness.

These ranker versions of his tape transcripts, though, Hoover was now circulating among the upper echelons of the executive branch under the new president, Lyndon Johnson. But Johnson himself, despite having as deep-gullied a country drawl as any Southerner in Washington, was rather more expansive of spirit than Hoover could have supposed and — aware as well that the file on King was more or less the same sort of squalid business Hoover had been conducting on all of them over the years — disappointed the director, as had the Kennedys, by declining to repudiate King. Certain House members of the more crustacean conservative variety began complaining to Attorney General Kennedy that Hoover had let them know that King was a Communist debauchee but the Justice Department was restraining him from spreading that alarm about. Actually, confidential indications of what the tapes contained and offers to provide select excerpts were being discreetly tendered by FBI agents to a number of chosen newsmen — including parties at the TV news networks, editors at the *Atlanta Constitution*, *Newsweek*'s Washington bureau chief Ben Bradlee — but, remarkably, none of this proffered material found its way into their reportage, a restraint virtually inconceivable in these times, meaning, of course, that King would very likely never have survived now as the figure he was then.

Nevertheless, word of these attempted leaks was not long in reaching King, leaving him deeply shaken. It was as if, his libidinous compulsions having delivered him into Hoover's hands, Hoover had now become the agent releasing back upon him all the demons of his guilts. Hoover himself, smarting over the absence of any open reaction to the colossal public scam he felt King was pulling off, finally chose to hold an interview with a group of women reporters, in which he snapped out that King was "the most notorious liar" and "one of the lowest characters in the country," who was "controlled" by Communist agents to boot. It seemed at the time a puzzlingly vehement expostulation from the FBI director, and King merely responded with a studiedly serene statement that the director "has apparently faltered under the awesome burden, complexities and responsibilities of his office. . . . I have nothing but sympathy for this man who has served his country so well." Considerably less serene, however, were the private scrimmagings by the SCLC and some in the administration to arrange a personal meeting of possible conciliation between King and a decidedly reluctant Hoover. When Hoover finally consented, King arrived at his office markedly tense, accompanied by three aides, and the session went stiffly, somewhat apologetically on King's part for any "misrepresentations" of his regard for the FBI. These apparent attempts by King to appease him with professions of respect Hoover received in somewhat the same bland manner he would receive at breakfast a properly repoached egg and then set it down for his dog. Hoover then swung into a monologue, lasting for about an hour, about the Bureau's irreproachable past performances. It was, for him, merely an obligatory ceremony of counterfeit politeness that hardly ended things at all.

But King had found something immediately, instinctively cheering about Lyndon Johnson — this huge, ponderous, hill country Texan, oversize of ego, exuberances, aspirations, who wanted only to be the greatest president in the history of the Republic, and who administered the capacious-hearted generosities of his War on Poverty and Great Society benefactions with the same swooping eagerness with which he would impress visitors to his ranch into smacking down large dispensations of buttermilk. In a private session at the White House shortly after assuming the presidency, Johnson gustily assured King and other civil rights leaders that he now meant to get passed "without a word or comma changed" Kennedy's public accommodations bill — which, his presence and persuasions like some prodigious force of raw nature, he speedily achieved, though voicing afterward to his staff what had been Kennedy's own fear, "I think we just gave the South to the Republicans." But out of his compulsion to personally straw-boss the entire course of the country, Johnson somewhat dismayed King by discouraging any further demonstrations, insisting that his administration could now be counted on to secure the rights of African Americans in full.

As was the case, the dramatic high definition given the nonviolent movement by Birmingham and then the Washington March had, over the months since, been rapidly wasting away — and SNCC's angrier activists were swarming into the emptiness, opening up a new front in Mississippi. Their swashbucklingly militant style had become increasingly intriguing to civil rights sympathizers in the North, to the extent that James Bevel warned his SCLC colleagues, "People are losing faith in the nonviolent movement." With their Alabama voter registration initiative still far from fully formed, the SCLC began casting about again for a major campaign in the interim to give the nonviolent principle another telling victory.

It was that urgency that impelled King and the SCLC finally into St. Augustine, Florida.

★ ★ ★

The oldest city in America, with the oldest record of slave trafficking from its beginnings as a Spanish settlement over fifty years before Jamestown, St. Augustine in 1964 was a carefully tended seaside tourist museum of a town whose citizens lived mostly off the vestiges of its Spanish past, which included the relic of its old slave market at one end of its palm-fringed square. But under its curio quaintness, St. Augustine was a grim testimonial to how, as King had been maintaining, rights won in law still had to be actively, sometimes agonizingly, rewon in reality on the ground. For most of its white citizenry and the city authorities, along with the population of white razorback toughs inhabiting its surrounding expanses of stump-smoldering timberland and potato fields, it was as if nothing whatsoever had transpired during the nine years since Montgomery. A local black movement had ventured small demonstrations to press appeals, forlornly familiar by now, for the desegregation of all public and civic facilities, hiring opened to blacks in the city's government and businesses, the creation of a biracial council. But these petitions had been answered only by recurring runs of vigilante violence, frontyard cross burnings and shotgun blasts at black homes, the car of one black family set ablaze and the house of another. Sensitive to the disarray in its tourist trade these disturbances could occasion, the city commission did once again agree to a conference with local black leaders, but when the black deputation entered the commission chamber at the appointed time, they found only a tape recorder resting on an empty table, a city functionary instructing them to speak their grievances into the machine for later consideration by the commissioners.

King's SCLC moved in finally in the late spring of 1964 for a campaign — which I would eventually be sent down as a novice correspondent for *Newsweek* to cover — that was timed to coincide with St. Augustine's quadracentennial anniversary commemoration. The strategy, learned from Albany's debacle and applied in Birmingham, was to besiege the more vulnerable economic interests into exacting concessions from recalcitrant political officials. But they found St. Augustine unique among the sites of racial conflict in the South: in contrast even with Birmingham, where Bull Connor had at least succeeded in persuading the Klan to hold at bay for a while to let him operate, St. Augustine had by the summer reeled into a dizzy limbo of all law, with its police acting not so much to avert as to supervise and abet its popular sprees of violence.

It was generally understood that the sheriff, a plump, balding, beak-nosed fellow by the name of L. O. (for "Look Out!" to blacks in the city) Davis, was an active accomplice of the especially virulent local Klan contingent, which pleasantly called itself the Ancient City Hunting Club, its members regularly seen lounging about his office. In fact, Davis effectively shared enforcement powers for repelling demonstrations with the Hunting Club's chieftain, whom he had coached long ago in high school football — a pig farmer and sometime bootlegger named Holstead "Hoss" Manucy, a heavy heap of a figure with an affably beaming sun-singed ham of a face, who happily informed me once in his fog-throated wheeze, "I ain't got no bad habits. Don't smoke, don't cuss. My only bad habit is fightin' nigguhs." Commanding a force of some thousand irregulars equipped with citizens band radios and an artillery of shotguns and deer rifles, Manucy had completely immobilized with fear the community's middle mass of white citizens and businessmen. One more liberally inclined white resident lamented, "The only difference down here between the mob and the police is the police are the ones with the hats on."

In the mornings came the melees at the segregated beaches. Lined along the sand beside the road would be a ragamuffin fleet of battered cars, miniature dime-store Confederate flags snapping from their aerials in the sea wind, with a pack of shirtless and barefooted young whites leaning against them with an assortment of their shower-sandaled women, waiting for that day's detachment of demonstrators to arrive. When they did, huddled close together in their bathing suits, they were set upon with fists, kicks, and clubs, with the police moving forward simply to encircle the violence. There was a certain female shrillness peculiar to these assaults: lank, sun-cured women in checkered men's shirts and Crayola-bright pedal pushers supplied a sort of Eumenidean chorus of shrieks — "Hoo*ieee*, git 'em, boys!" — and, if women were among the demonstrators, flung themselves on them in a swirl of hair, skirts, clawings, lungs going like a battle of cats.

Then, after sundown, the night marches would set out from a church in the black section toward the Old Slave Market on the town's square, where often the Klan was holding its own rally, addressed by an itinerant drummer of racist rant named, aptly enough, Connie Lynch, a wiry little man in a Wyatt Earp string tie braying out of the side of his mouth into a bullhorn, "This here Martin Lucifer Coon, somebody ought to tell him *white* men wrote the Constitution for *white* people, not for these black varmints out there whose relatives in Africa are still invitin' the neighbors over for supper and puttin' them into the stewpot." The marchers then, their singing and clapping abruptly subsiding into a spooky shuffling silence under a full summer moon as they arrived at the square, would move on into a chaos of mayhem from the hundreds of whites mobbed there. At one point, a deputy to Robert Kennedy was dispatched down to St. Augustine, but he reported back that the city was simply too riotous for any mediation attempts at all.

In his movements in and out of the city through those summer weeks, King had already been arrested once, with nine others, when they presented themselves to be served at a motel restaurant. At a news conference later, King declared that efforts to get the Justice Department to step forcefully into St. Augustine to protect marchers had met only with bland noncomittals, and he warned that "it may well be we will have to place our bodies as sacrifices if we don't get protection." In fact, King was increasingly proclaiming at mass meetings in St. Augustine his readiness to die, that "if physical death is the price I must pay to free my white brother and all my brothers and sisters from a permanent death of the spirit, then nothing can be more redemptive." Indeed, his assassination seemed a real possibility hanging in the air, and when King was in the city, he would be shifted from house to house, armed guards posted wherever he was staying. One late afternoon, though, I happened to come upon him strolling casually in his shirtsleeves, seemingly out of nowhere, down a sidewalk in the black section, holding the hand of his six-year-old son, Martin Luther King III, with nobody else around him. He stopped to tell me, "This is the most lawless city I've ever been in, I've never seen this kind of wide-open violence." As soon as his presence was discovered there, people came clustering around him, and his aides shortly arrived. As he conferred with them off beside the curb, he paused once to glance down at his small son and murmur, "Now, don't you go wandering off, Marty. You stay close to Daddy here."

It was the next night — though Florida's governor had by now thought it prudent to dispatch state troopers into the vacuum of law in St. Augustine — that the square was engulfed in a full-blown maelstrom of savagery. Just after sunset, with a Klan rally again in progress at the Old Slave Market, a march led by Vivian and Shuttlesworth came around the corner down the street and began heading up alongside the square, with Lynch shrilling, "There they are! Here come the niggers now!" And with a thunderous volley of rebel yells, the whole crowd — some eight hundred strong — streamed toward them under the palms. Separated at first from the marchers by a waist-high hedge and, on the other side of that, a cordon of state troopers with German shepherds, the mob seethed, dammed for a moment, but from it trash-can lids began lofting through the darkness, followed then by the trash cans themselves, then park benches, then the cement saucer of a bird-bath actually heaved somehow over the police. The marchers were proceeding now two abreast, shrinking as closely together as possible, on through this mad bombardment, with the crowd still contained inside the hedges of the square washing after them as they turned at its far end and started down the other side, heading now with a mute and accelerating haste back toward the black section. And at this point — with a wail from the women, "Don't let 'em git away, boys, *go git 'em!*" — the mob, bringing out tire tools and bats and logging chains and even several cue-stick handles, went howling over the hedges.

The whole block of the square was now drowned in a roar, driving and mindless and unstoppable, that seemed to be coming not from human throats, but from some enormous and monstrous presence hovering right overhead in the night, with a rapid underbeating of dull thuds. In a frenzied barking of police dogs, whites were whirling everywhere, seemed to cover everything, snatching blacks out of the march and hammering at them with down-swinging fists like carnies driving tent stakes. One tall, gangling woman, looking as if she were being sucked up a jet engine, her arms flailing and hair flying, charged screechingly into a huddle of young black girls. It had all become a formless, hopeless butchery, and the state troopers were quickly occupied with clubbing back ambushes on themselves, whites they were trying to arrest yanked out of their arms and out of patrol cars, plowing charges sending troopers toppling back with startled grunts, "*God*dammit to hell sonuvabitchin' *bastard*. . . ." The marchers, tossed back and forth by successive stampeding attacks, retreated in a kind of faltering rush, strangely soundless themselves, eyes merely staring almost drowsily straight ahead — but some at last started to run, then all of them, suddenly running wordless through the howl around them.

It was a few moments later that, following them back into the black section, I saw King standing alone and unnoticed in the shadows of a front porch, watching them stumbling past him in the dim shine of the streetlights like the tattered remnant of a brigade filtering back from a battlefield disaster, girls in shredded clothes, sobs now lifting up from them, a few scattered screams like a long-pent breath at last released — he watching them with that stricken expression of amazement, horror, but also captivation. . . . Meanwhile, C. T. Vivian was hurrying at a panting trot around the neighborhood, trying to restrain the small parties of young blacks forming on street corners to return to the square with their guns. For those few minutes, St. Augustine was tottering on the edge of outright racial war, with one black woman, a bandage over one eye, crying out over the street — only one of the echoes of Malcolm rising around King these days — "They done it now. I say, if we got to fight, dammit, *fight!* If we got to die, dammit, *die!* To hell with this nonviolence!" Vivian finally found King at the center of a seethe of people on the sidewalk beside the grimy brick church from which the march had set out, and he leaned to yell in his ear over the noise, "You've got to get them back in the church!" Someone opened the door of a car along the curb, and King stepped up into it; then, braced by hands from behind, he lifted his arms and called: "Please, everybody! Everybody, listen! We must go into the church, everybody, let's all come into the church now for a few minutes." As most of the crowd began moving slowly up the church's cement steps, King stepped down from the opened car door and muttered to Andrew Young, "I need to find a telephone. This has been terrible. Find me a phone. . . ."

Inside the church, there transpired then one of those quiet miracles of the nonviolent movement. Under sluggishly twirling ceiling fans, the crowd settled into the pews with a tense, outraged, impatient rustling, while a teenage girl cringed in a back corner with her face to the wall, still sobbing hysterically, as an old woman simply, silently fanned her with a cardboard fan. Abernathy took the pulpit, and in one of those moments that helped explain why King would not part with him, he rumbled out as he swabbed at his heavy, sweat-slick face with a white handkerchief, "What happened tonight was one of the dark hours of our movement. You have passed through it. Their purpose is to break your spirit, to break your heart. But let them beat us, let them kick us — we will *continue* to present our bodies in peaceful witness for justice, we ain't gonna let *nobody* turn us 'round. And we will *not* turn to hate, we gonna keep on lovin' Mr. L. O. Davis and his cops and Klansmen, we gonna love this whole hate-filled city of St. Augustine right on into freedom and righteousness, 'cause we are *all* the children of God here together on this earth!" This brought a clamor of amens, a stirring of applause, and Abernathy led them then into an old, slowly rolling hymn that, as it gathered over the sanctuary, became like a calm, sweet wind of approaching rain breathing over that gloweringly hot and bitter night: *God will take care of you . . . in every way all through the day . . . God will take ca-are of you. . . .* As the singing swelled out to the sidewalks in front

213

of the church, young blacks still moiling loudly under the streetlights grew quiet and listened — even as cars were pulling away, bearing the last of the injured to the hospital. So were that night's sweltering fevers for vengeance translated back into the higher, finally mysterious will to love despite everything, something Malcolm never could understand, that was the peculiar genius and power King had brought to the movement. Another reporter at the church that evening remarked, "What those white hot-rods back at the square don't realize is that Martin Luther King is the best friend they ever had. Whole lot of rednecks walking the streets today wouldn't be if it weren't for him."

King himself, though — sitting with loosened tie and shirt sopped with sweat in the darkened front parlor, where he was waiting to get a call through to the Justice Department to plead for protective federal intervention — had confessed at one point in a low and weary voice, "Yes, when things happen like this tonight, you question sometimes, *What are we doing to these people?*" A glass of ice water wrapped in a paper napkin was brought to him from the kitchen, and sipping from it, he leaned forward, talking with Shuttlesworth, Young, Abernathy now, repeatedly running one hand back over his head and then letting it hang at the back of his neck as he told them, "It can't go on like this. It's awful. It just can't go on like this. . . ."

But it did. For all its Grand Guignol sound and fury, St. Augustine was to welter on to only another indecisive effort for King — his strategic equation from Birmingham breaking down here. The white business community, instead of being compelled by the turmoil to constrain concessions from the civic powers, simply availed itself of the violence to keep balking on negotiations, citing fear of the savagery loose in the streets. A federal judge did impose more sober strictures on the behavior of St. Augustine's law officials and ordered a desegregation of public businesses in the city, but after its governing commission voted to comply with the newly passed Public Accommodations Law, an aide to President Johnson reported back to Washington, they had reverted to resegregating the city, still "claiming they were afraid." Despite King's earlier vows not to leave St. Augustine until its segregationist system was dismantled, "even if it means physical death," a certain inflationary factor was setting into such repeated dire proclamations of his by now, and he was reduced there to the minimal appeal of at least a biracial committee, which a grand jury did go about appointing — only to have all its white members resign. In the end, St. Augustine wound up an endeavor alarmingly close to the futility of Albany, precisely the sort of misfire the SCLC's nonviolent operation could least afford at the time.

That same summer, over in Mississippi, a far more sweeping offensive was under way, launched over the whole expanse of that most forbidding of the inner South's states by a coalition of activist cadres from SNCC, the Congress for Racial Equality, even the NAACP, that called itself the Council of Federated Organizations (COFO). Already there for three years, since leaving the SCLC for SNCC, had been the solitary movement mystic Bob Moses, quietly and obscurely toiling at voter registration, living with local black families, repeatedly beaten and arrested, his slight, coveralled, bespectacled, ethereal figure having taken on within the movement virtually a sacred mystique. Now in the COFO summer of 1964, legions of other young circuit riders, white and black, including about a thousand student volunteers from the North and the West Coast, had journeyed down into the dark glamours of that state of legendary racial feudalism and violence. They ranged out into the remotest back stretches of its naturally brooding and tragic landscapes to conduct civic education projects for blacks in Freedom Schools and a voter registration campaign ultimately directed toward the creation of a new, egalitarian political party in the state, the Mississippi Freedom Democratic Party (MFDP).

It was a summer, to be sure, not without its poetries — mass meetings in a flimsy little pine-plank church out in the remote reaches of a Mississippi midsummer night with light glowing through its cracks like a shuttered lantern, while inside a dense congregation of blacks, a seemingly sourceless and magical conjuration out of the empty moonlit spaces of the countryside, sang with a glad blare old spirituals transported now to this live edge of history, *Paul and Silas bound in jail, didn't have no money for to go their bail. . . . Keep yo eyes on the prize, hold on!* . . . What this lyric COFO crusade into Mississippi meant to bring to pass, finally, was nothing less than a democratic civilizing of that primeval recess of the nation. And not surprisingly, it was received by the state's native whites with about the cordiality expressed by one waitress who volunteered with a hissing sincerity to a tableful of reporters in a Jackson restaurant, "I'd just like to take a machine gun and mow away every single one of those COFO things." It indeed turned out a long and vicious summer of beatings, mob maulings, bombings, church burnings, night raids on the ramshackle Freedom Houses out in the scrubby little towns where COFO workers were lodged. Early on, in June, three of those workers — two of them white, Andrew Goodman and Michael Schwerner, and a local black youth, James Chaney — disappeared one night in the little central Mississippi town of Philadelphia, their bullet-riddled bodies found some two months later in a cattle-pond dam.

King, toiling in the coils of St. Augustine, had remained largely marginal so far to the vaster drama playing itself out in Mississippi. But in the midst of that dangerous summer, Bob Moses invited him to make a sojourn in the state for a tour of COFO projects — Moses himself, despite his own defection from the SCLC, still appreciating the singularly energizing effect King's simple presence would work on the desolated and terrorized spirit of Mississippi's blacks. With an immediate flurry of reports that the Klan intended to kill him while he was there, King, before leaving, allowed to Coretta and aides with a matter-of-fact resignation that he did not expect to survive the trip. For some reason, such fatal contemplations seemed to be crowding his mind more and more since St. Augustine, and it was as if, with his failure there, he longed to throw himself into this open maw of mortal peril in Mississippi.

His first stop was in Greenwood, on the edge of the Delta, the hometown of Byron De La Beckwith, who had gone through two hung juries in trials for his ambush murder of Medgar Evers. On a steamy afternoon just after a heavy, leaden rain, as King set out on a walk through Greenwood's black section, it became immediately evident, just as Moses had recognized, how much he remained a mythic figure still to the masses of America's blacks. Proceeding coatless, in a cool white shirt, along the narrow dirt lanes, he leaned in the opened doors of honky-tonks and cafés to invite everyone to the rally that night for the Mississippi Freedom Democratic Party — "Yes, well, hope to see yawl at the meetin' tonight" — with the faces in the gloom inside staring astonished at his sudden translation before them out of distant glory. As he walked on along the closely cluttered rows of paintless slumped shanties, their ragtag fences enclosing paltry grassless yards under chinaberry trees, the front porches filled rapidly as he passed, people calling quietly to others, "It's Dr. King! Dr. King out here! Yeah, *'tis,* c'mere, lookahere, it's Dr. King!" Upon reaching the New Savoy Cafe, he stood on a crude plank bench above the crowd now collected around him, proclaiming to them in his familiar rolling resonations, "Mississippi has treated the Negro as if he is a thing instead of a person. But you must not allow *anybody* to make you feel you are not significant and you do not count. Every Negro here in Greenwood, Mississippi, has worth and dignity — because white, Negro, Chinese, Indian, man or woman or child, we are all the children of God. You are *somebody*. I want every one of you to say that out loud now to yourself — *I am somebody.*" And as he repeated it several times, he was answered by a strangely dreamlike murmuration from the crowd, *I am — somebody. . . .*

That evening, as if in direct counter to that proposition of King's, while he was conducting the MFDP rally in a black church, the Klan flew a small single-engine plane over the town, sprinkling down mimeographed leaflets asserting that the community's blacks would still be "just as ignorant, just as dumb, and just as foul-smelling" after King departed. But to the fifteen hundred Greenwood black citizens who had turned out for the mass meeting that night, King orated, "We have a power that's greater than all the guns in Greenwood or the state of Mississippi, a power greater than all the guns and bombs of all the armies in the world. We have the power of our *souls!*" Yet, in the booming ovation to this, one could also hear, coming from several SNCC partisans ranged around the back of the church, the by now familiar hoots of that disaffection and alienation, that Malcolm mood, steadily collecting against King: "Oh, de Lawd! De *Lawd,* now!"

Finally, King journeyed to the small hamlet of Philadelphia itself, from which Schwerner, Goodman, and Chaney had been abducted, their bodies not yet found. Walking the hilly, pebbled, orange-dirt lanes of the black quarter there, King paused on a corner to remark to me, "That old man I was talking to back there a moment ago, I could see the fear in his eyes. They've been living in such a paralyzing fear here all their lives. And in a way, it can be liberating for them just to see me moving openly about the community, you know, a Negro openly calling for their freedom walking around here in the streets of Philadelphia, and not being afraid."

"Are you, though?" I asked.

"Humh." He merely looked away. But when he offered his hand a few minutes later in parting, it was, in the fierce heat of that morning, surprisingly cold and dank.

The brave aspirations of that COFO summer ended up, though, stripping the gears of reality when, in late August, an MFDP delegation traveled to the Democratic convention in Atlantic City to challenge the seating of Mississippi's all-white delegation of party regulars. King gamely joined them there to lobby on behalf of their claim for official acceptance as the state's only democratically legitimate party, however woefully naive he suspected it to be. But having been duly chosen in their own local caucuses, assuming they had played by all the political rules, "it never occurred to us," one MFDP member would later maintain, "that our delegation would be turned down." Johnson, however, who had passed by now into his Caesar phase, had a monumental phobia about his nominating convention being disrupted by a civil rights rhubarb that could insure the loss of an already unsteady South to Barry Goldwater, and he instructed vice presidential hopeful Hubert Humphrey and other party deputies to dispose of the fret. The MFDP delegation was incensed by the compromise arrangement then proposed to them: to give two of them "at large" votes and the sixty-two others to be seated as "guests" of the convention, with a pledge to eliminate any racial discrimination in the state's delegation to the next convention. King, though, in the rowdy free-for-all discussions that followed, was reluctant to advise the MFDP to refuse the offer, considering it still a notable advance from the situation prevailing beforehand; finally he suggested that, as a national civil rights strategist, he would "want you to take this," acknowledging, however, that "if I were a Mississippi Negro, I would vote against it." But to many in SNCC, King had simply confirmed once again his bourgeois moderate's readiness to betray principle for the sake of not estranging himself from the system. Bob Moses spoke up, with a clarity that seemed to shame King's pained ambivalences: "We're not here to bring politics to our morality. We're here to bring morality to our politics." The MFDP delegation voted to spurn the compromise and returned forthwith to Mississippi.

However hopeless an adventure of political romanticism it had all been, the Atlantic City episode became the pivotal, conclusive disillusionment among the movement's more hot-wired militants about what could ever be expected of America's ruling political order and its putatively liberal viceroys like Humphrey. One veteran of COFO's Mississippi summer termed it "the end of innocence," after which "things could never be the same." Stokely Carmichael decreed, "If you try to work from within, you're going to get cheated. The only way the Negro can be effective is to wreak havoc from without." Bob Moses himself soon withdrew from the movement altogether, paying a call one morning to an old friend, Ed King, the chaplain at interracial Tougaloo College on the outskirts of Jackson, who had been perhaps closer to Moses than any other white through Moses's years in Mississippi. But Moses now commenced to inform King, in his soft, shy voice, that he had concluded that the values and vitality of all white society were exhausted and bankrupt, and therefore black people had nothing to gain but a similar corruption and emptiness from integration with whites, that in fact white civilization would inevitably cave in on itself over time — and finally, that this would be the last conversation in which he would ever engage with a white.

One writer for a New York magazine who had followed Moses for some time remarked, "He has the most excruciatingly moral sense I have ever seen in a man. He is really too moral for this world." Through the following years, Moses floated about, from the South to Africa and back to Cambridge and Harvard, even changing his last name to Parris for a while, finally returning to Mississippi to teach math in a Jackson high school — one of the ghosts of that distant, brief, lightning-vivid time of belief and violence and courage, that eloquence of the human spirit once in the South during the movement.

After the summer of 1964, King was left trying to navigate between Moses's moral purities and, in denunciations of him by SNCC, Malcolm's kind of anger — aware that in that anger was some terrible but as yet unaddressed truth. At the same time, reports kept filtering to him of J. Edgar Hoover's attempts to smuggle FBI intelligence about his sexual gambols into the general public attention. If Hoover succeeded, King well knew it could instantly demolish his moral standing and seriously stagger the movement itself. Harried now from multiple sides, confronted yet again after Birmingham and the Washington March by the evanescence of all renown, King that autumn, stunned with exhaustion, checked into an Atlanta hospital with a viral fever.

It was in this low ebb of circumstances that, early one morning, he was awakened in his hospital room by a call from Coretta: it had just been announced that, for his nonviolent civil rights ministry since Montgomery, he had been awarded the 1964 Nobel Peace Prize. Exhilaration at the wonder and spectacular reaffirmation of this news wholly restored him. When Coretta and several aides arrived in his room, he conducted them all in a prayer of thanksgiving for this "foremost of earthly honors" accorded not just to him but to their movement. To the reporters who congregated at the hospital, he had returned enough to his old assurance of high purpose to resound, "History has thrust me in this position. . . . It would be both immoral and a sign of ingratitude if I did not face my moral responsibility to do what I can in this struggle."

Hoover, however — as he had earlier grumped about a King visit to the Vatican, "I am amazed that the Pope gave an audience to such a degenerate" — now decried to his staff the farce of such a "top alley cat" being dignified with a Nobel Prize. And despite his initial elation, King made the trip to Norway to receive the prize, accompanied by Coretta and a rather copious entourage, again heavy with anxiety about the threat of Hoover's disclosures: At one point during the flight, he blurted to a white associate that while he had trespassed in grievous sensual ways in the past, he was resolved to abstain from those indulgences from now on. Though those transgressions steadfastly remained to Coretta no more than foul gossip, she would later acknowledge "how depressed he was during the entire Nobel trip. It was a time when he ought to have been happy" but "was worried that the rumors might hurt the movement," and "the public never knew what he was going through."

Neither was King particularly cheered when, at the hotel in Oslo where he and his party were lodged, Abernathy and his wife raised repeated rows about unequal accommodations, and the hotel's security delicately complained about the frolicking of some in his retinue, featuring one late-night gallop down a corridor by the nude figure of his brother, A.D., in pursuit of an Oslo nymph of the evening he protested had stolen his money. But on one occasion through the series of ceremonies, Daddy King arose for a personal celebration, lifting a toast, tearfully, "to God" for bringing him up out of a south Georgia sharecropper's farm to give to the world this son, only praying now "that God will keep him safe." Still, not until a party later in Stockholm did King bestir himself out of his gloom, for at least one buoyant moment, to dance a waltz with Coretta, a waltz that yet had a faintly wistful and elegiac air — the first time they had danced together since their courtship over eleven years earlier (but amazingly only eleven years) as students in Boston.

On his return to Atlanta, though, King was still so oppressed of spirit that, one evening, he disappeared without a word, and a boyhood friend who was now an Atlanta police officer, after an alarmed call from King's family, finally found him around midnight outside a plant where a bitter labor conflict had been under way for weeks over racial wage discriminations — King simply standing alone on the sidewalk in the dark, waiting to talk to the black workers on a shift change.

All along there had persevered in King a

kind of secret desperation not to lose touch with that exaltation, that God-communion, of his midnight kitchen epiphany in Montgomery. One acquaintance would later tell biographer David Garrow about coming across King once shut alone in a closet, on his knees, praying. But part of that passionate earnestness, lasting ever since his boyhood gestures at suicide over dismay about his grandmother, had been his extravagant capacity for guilt: several years after passing by a hitchhiker on a deserted road one night, he was still agonizing over it to his Ebenezer congregation: "I didn't stop to help the man because I was afraid." As one writer would later observe, for King an answer to his guilt seemed to be to turn anger on himself "as punishment for this guilt. . . . There was some deep compulsion in King to suffer, to sacrifice himself." With the vast store of guilt he had now compiled with his sexual careering, duly transcribed by the dour recording angel of Hoover's FBI, his death had become all the more constant an obsession with him, as if it were the only way to exorcise that guilt and, at the same time, lift him beyond the din of disaffected angers around him and into the completion and fulfillment of that moral heroic promise opened up to him in Montgomery.

Those closest to King had grown increasingly concerned that he could come to be immured in this morbid fixation. But even as mobilizations were taking final shape for the SCLC's new voter registration campaign in Selma, King insistently warned them all, as Coretta would remember, that "somebody was going to get killed in Selma," that "he didn't expect us to get out of Selma without bloodshed."

III

As early as Montgomery, King had foreseen that, in the end, "the chief weapon in our fight for civil rights is the vote" and declared at a Washington rally during that beginning time, "Do you realize what would happen . . . if three million Negro voters were added to the rolls in the South?" Now, in 1964, in Alabama alone some half million black citizens were still unregistered, nearly 80 percent of the state's black voting-age population, and over four million more across the rest of the South. The implications for a transfiguration of the South's whole political character were stupendous.

Invited to drop by the White House after

his Nobel Prize trip, King posed to Johnson, now president in his own right after his Johnson-size clobbering of Goldwater, the urgent need for substantial federal legislation to secure voting rights for blacks in the South. But Johnson, while assuring King such legislation was already in the works, insisted that it would be an impossibility to get it passed in Congress right now, so soon after enactment of the Public Accommodations Law.

But Young and others in the SCLC were contending that, with the Public Accommodations Law meeting with a surprising compliance over most of the South, it was imperative to move on to the finishing business now of voter registration. And as Birmingham had finally prevailed to produce a public accommodations bill from a deeply disinclined Kennedy, Selma would be a campaign premeditated to force voting rights legislation from Johnson — a campaign set in a county where fewer than 250 of the 15,000 blacks of voting age were registered. On the second day of the new year of 1965, then, King arrived in Selma for the first of what would become a marathon series of mass meetings over the weeks ahead in the brick citadel of Brown Chapel AME Church, trumpeting out through those days and nights that "to get the right to vote everywhere in Alabama . . . [w]e must be ready to march. We must be ready to go to jail by the thousands. . . . We will bring a voting bill into being on the streets of Selma!"

But King's SCLC again faced, as in Albany and Birmingham, a dispersion of authority among Selma's white officials. The new mayor, Joe Smitherman, a young refrigerator salesman of supposedly milder segregationist tenor, and his businesslike police chief, Wilson Baker, were both determined to employ Laurie Pritchett's tactic (insidious still, that Albany precedent) of genial-mannered resistance. But Baker was constantly tussling over jurisdictional lines with the county sheriff, Jim Clark, a beefy, Big Buster lawman with a flashing temper, in whom the SCLC found it had likely lucked upon another Bull Connor. Sporting on his sheriff's jacket a large button lettered "Never," Clark offered a simple response to demonstrators, directing his deputies and volunteer posse to have at them with night-sticks and, in place of Connor's fire hoses, electric cattle prods, with which he and his men once herded some 165 young protesters all the way out of Selma into the open countryside at a jogging trot for about three miles.

Through the chill dull weathers of late winter, then, into the raw edge of spring, marches regularly wound through Selma's low flat streets to the courthouse, where Clark and his deputies systematically rebuffed their demands to register to vote and arrested them — Clark now and then personally pitching in to scuffle with them himself, taking his nightstick to one hefty middle-aged defiant woman who, no Rosa Parks, slugged him. Eventually King too was arrested, by Wilson Baker, and fasting in jail, steadily sent out notes to Andrew Young entreating that he not allow any lull in the tempo of demonstrations. For one thing, King was wary of the ever-present threat that the SNCC forces also in Selma might with their hasty heats bear away the nonviolent spirit of the campaign. Then, while he was still in jail, there happened to appear in Selma none other than Malcolm X.

As Malcolm's engagement with the larger world around him had been steadily widening, so had his restlessness within the confines of the Black Muslims' righteous ghetto, climaxed by his devastating discovery that the Muslims' elderly leader, Elijah Muhammad, had been dallying with a succession of young secretaries, some of

233

whom had already borne what Muhammad's inner court decorously referred to as "divine babies." As word of Malcolm's disaffection spread within the Muslim community, he found himself stalked now by the Nation's own Fruit of Islam enforcers. It was almost certainly to a degree in flight from all this that he set out on a pilgrimage to Mecca, during which, among its myriad races, he came by the liberating enlightenment that, as he professed when he returned, "the white man is *not* inherently evil, but America's racist society influences him to act evilly."

Well before this, actually, despite his beratings of the civil rights movement, Malcolm had been stirred by the spectacle it presented as the most powerful mass drama then unfolding in the black community, and he now could be frequently seen looming tall and alone at the margins of its rallies and demonstrations. Though he still could not bring himself to accept the ethic of nonviolence, Malcolm was in "a period of explosive and chaotic growth," one of his most discerning biographers, Peter Goldman, would later observe, "re-creating himself on the run." He announced that it had become his new calling "to help create a society in which there could exist honest white–black brotherhood" and, ultimately, "to change this miserable condition that exists on this earth." In fact, from his wretched beginnings, at no point in his life could Malcolm cease struggling, by some dim but resistless instinct, upward for more light.

But he had wandered now into a kind of indefinite zone, suspended between the blank furies of his past and his still unformed mission for some more hopeful future, and despite his lurching attempts to reach out to them, he was still rejected by the mainline civil rights movement. Once, during the demonstrations in St. Augustine, Malcolm had sent a telegram to King, informing him that on his word, "we will immediately dispatch some of our brothers there to organize our people into self-defense units . . . and the Ku Klux Klan will receive a taste of its own medicine." King was appalled at the idea.

Now while King was in jail in Selma, Malcolm had been invited by SNCC, for its own mischievous designs, to address a mass meeting there. He wound up seated on the podium beside Coretta, and he presently leaned close to whisper to her — with what Coretta would later recall as a somehow poignantly apologetic eagerness — "to let Martin know he was not causing trouble or making it difficult, but that he was trying to make it easier" by simply presenting his notorious image to whites as the "alternative" to King's appeal. It was as though he were striving to enter on his own into a kind of collaboration with King.

But his past would not turn him loose. Still tracked by Muslim street soldiers, Malcolm told friends they could be trusted to deliver on their lethal purposes "because I taught them myself." Only a few weeks after his message to Coretta at that mass meeting in Selma, when Malcolm, rising to speak to his few lingering faithful in Harlem's Audubon Ballroom, was slain in a bedlam of gunfire, it was as if he had been ambushed by his own hand, by the old rages of his past.

King declared afterward that he was "deeply saddened and appalled" by "the brutal assassination of Malcolm X," tragically coming as it had when Malcolm was "moving toward a greater understanding of the nonviolent movement and toward more tolerance of white people." But his death hardly ended the tensions between their old duality of visions. Ironically, it was to be Malcolm's fierce earlier persona, his slayer, as it were — Malcolm during his Muslim days of finger-spearing racial malediction, the nemesis of white America — to which his subsequent following would fasten, and which would increasingly imperil King's dream of a common, egalitarian American neighborhood, his furious and unforgiving voice still calling out in the firestorms of wrath to come in America's inner cities, "Do you know why the white man really hates you? It's because every time he sees your face he sees a mirror of his crime."

King, of course, had carried into Selma his own fatal forebodings. Abernathy later quoted him as confiding once, while they were driving to Selma, "I'm sure it will be in Selma. This is the time and place." For its part, the FBI had decided by now it would no longer notify him of death threats against him that came to its attention, a consideration it extended to most other public figures, but would at the most merely refer them to local authorities to attend to as they may, or may not, see fit.

More, frustrated in his efforts to expose King's carnal delinquencies, Hoover — having learned from the wiretaps of King's distress about his investigations — elected to strike more directly. Just as the Selma campaign was getting under way, Coretta happened to open a package, later to be called the "FBI suicide kit," addressed to King at the SCLC office, that held a reel of tape, along with an anonymous letter that read in part, "King, look into your heart. You know that you are a complete fraud and a great liability to us Negroes . . . a dissolute, abnormal moral imbecile. . . . The American public, the church organizations that have been helping . . . will know you for what you are. . . . There is but one way out for you. You better take it before your filthy, abnormal fraudulent self is bared to the nation." On the tape, when Coretta played it, were excerpts from the FBI's recordings of King's lusty hotel room ribaldries with associates, interspersed with groans and shouts in King's voice of unmistakable sexual grapplings. Coretta would maintain afterward that "I couldn't make much of it, it was just a lot of mumbo jumbo," but she deciphered enough to give her husband a distraught call to come home. King, when he heard the tape, was rocked. He hurriedly summoned in his closest aides to listen to it — plain to them all now was the assiduous malice with which Hoover had been stalking King. "They are out to break me," he despaired to a friend.

By the end of winter in Selma, with demonstrations having coursed on for a month, Jim Clark's bumpkinish brutalities had still not been enough to precipitate a conclusive crisis like Birmingham's, and the city's black citizenry was beginning to weary under the effort. Partly to alleviate them, the SCLC had been contemplating a widening of the campaign to surrounding counties, where Wallace had deployed state troopers under Al Lingo to supplement the local police. In neighboring Perry County, a nighttime march to the courthouse in Marion was, when the streetlights suddenly went out, routed with clubs in the darkness by the police and troopers, with one black youth, Jimmie Lee Jackson, while trying to fend off the blows to his mother, shot fatally in the stomach.

Leaving Jackson's funeral in tears, James Bevel told a compatriot that he felt like just walking the fifty-four miles on to the capital in Montgomery to call Wallace to account — and once again, it was Bevel's spontaneous impulse for dramatic improvisation that would provide the decisive stroke. That night at a mass meeting in Brown Chapel, he arose to declare that, as Mordecai in the Old Testament had implored Esther to go to the Persian king to plead that her people be spared from an extermination plot, the king now in Alabama was George Wallace and "I must go see the king!" With the congregation thronging to their feet, he cried out, "Be prepared to walk to Montgomery! Be prepared to sleep on the highway!" Though King was still in New York meeting with supporters, Bevel proceeded to announce to reporters that a march would set out the next Sunday from Selma to Montgomery. On his own, with that instinct for a gambit of inspired recklessness that had always entranced King, Bevel had set loose an unstoppable popular momentum. But he and Hosea Williams phoned King to advise that he not lead the march, Wallace having vowed publicly that Lingo's troopers would "use whatever measures are necessary" to stop it.

On that cold, wind-slapping Sunday in early March, Hosea Williams and John Lewis led a column of around five hundred marchers from Brown Chapel to the Edmund Pettus Bridge that spanned the Alabama River, moving over its high arch to find on the other side, massed across the four-lane highway to Montgomery, Col. Al Lingo's state troopers and Sheriff Clark's mounted posse. What followed then was like a long tapestry of violence unfolding with a terrible inexorability — Lingo's troopers in gas masks trampling forward, marchers tumbling backward, men and women falling, clubs flailing with ringing *thonk*s, Lewis hit and going down, Clark's horsemen now clattering forward in a haze of tear gas in a Cossack-like charge, eventually chasing marchers all the way back to Brown Chapel. Some seventy demonstrators were injured, seventeen of them hospitalized. And it was all witnessed by the nation on that Sunday evening's television news.

Suddenly King had his second Birmingham. Johnson declared in a press conference a few days later, "What happened in Selma was an American tragedy. . . . It is wrong to do violence to peaceful citizens in the streets of their towns. It is wrong to deny any Americans the right to vote." And he announced that he would be submitting to Congress a voting rights bill the following Monday. At the same time, at a national call from King for a second attempt at a march to Montgomery, there converged into Selma a pilgrimage of young clerics, housewives, movement partisans, labor union stalwarts, college students, an assemblage resembling some cinematic mural of the American conscience of that time — among them, a white Unitarian minister from

Boston, James Reeb, who was waylaid one night outside a Selma café by a gang of whites with clubs and sticks. He shortly died of the beating.

But this second procession to Montgomery was abruptly forestalled when federal district judge Frank Johnson, a thornily rectitudinous man who was an old adversary of Wallace's and a sturdy civil rights constitutionalist for the movement in the past, unexpectedly indicated he would be issuing a restraining order on any further marches until a hearing on the legality of official efforts to stop them. Again King was thrown into the dilemma, with thousands now crowded into Selma for the march the next morning, of whether to defy the federal court authority on which the movement had long vitally relied. After deliberating through the night with administration emissaries John Doar and LeRoy Collins in the kitchen of the house where he was staying, King finally consented to the symbolic exercise of a march that, to avoid directly violating Johnson's order, would halt before reaching the state troopers barricading its way and then turn back toward Brown Chapel — an arrangement Lingo and Clark also agreed to. But when that day King led the marchers — two thousand of them now

— over the bridge and up to the ranked troopers, pausing for prayers and a singing of "We Shall Overcome" and then turning back toward the church, Lingo's troopers suddenly parted to open wide the highway to Montgomery, a maneuver obviously ordered by Wallace to embarrass King.

This "Tuesday Turnaround," as it was soon jeeringly called, did indeed produce much consternation among those unaware of King's reluctant compromise with Doar and Collins. In King's fumblings to explain it, he resorted to some outright dissembling, insisting that "no prearranged agreement existed," that simply "we agreed we would not break through the lines" and "knew we would not get to Montgomery." But among SNCC militants like James Forman, it brought resentments of King to an open derision, Forman denouncing him for performing "a classic example of trickery against the people."

Even so, the next Monday evening, when King watched President Johnson's televised presentation of the voting rights bill to Congress — in which Johnson declared in his whumping drawl that the recent scenes of the black American's "courage to risk safety and even to risk his life, have awakened the conscience of the nation" — it was like the highest confirmation yet, despite all the tribulations since Montgomery, of his original faith there: of the power of right, in open nonviolent confrontation with wrong, to rouse the larger community to shame and redress. Johnson went on, "It is not just Negroes, but really all of us, who must overcome the crippling legacy of bigotry and injustice. And *we shall overcome!*" At that line, King brimmed into tears, the first time any of his aides had ever seen him actually cry. Now the soul of the movement, in all the marches in country towns and tabernacle mass meetings over the South through these years, had at last found its way to the Office of the Presidency, sounded forth from there to the nation in the very accents of the South itself.

It was Selma Bridge that had really brought all this to pass, and in that sense, the Selma to Montgomery March that followed, after Judge Frank Johnson's court approval, was more a kind of celebratory pageant. Numbering three thousand when starting out for Selma, with King flanked by an array of religious and movement leaders, AFL-CIO officials, with assorted celebrities following behind, it was not unlike a recurrence of the Washington March, a year and a half later here in the inner reaches of Dixie, a processional constituting among other things a reaffirmation of King's Birmingham apotheosis. Proceeding by court order in daily stages of three hundred marchers, it trailed through Alabama's gusty spring drizzles, until, five days later reaching Montgomery after a heavy morning rain, it swelled to twenty-five thousand, welling on into the center of the city past Dexter Avenue Church, from which King had led, haltingly at first, the beginning of the movement only nine years ago, and surging on up to the front of Wallace's state capitol, which that movement was now challenging in a struggle that had amplified over all the South and begun to reach into the rest of the nation. With glimpses now and then of the vague figure of Wallace watching through the venetian blinds of his office, King's voice rang over the vast multitude before him, proclaiming that "we are standing before the forces of power in the state of Alabama, saying, 'We ain't gonna let nobody turn us around!' " He moved finally into a rendition of his refrain from Albany: "I know some of you are asking today, 'How long will it take?' . . . It will not be long. Because truth pressed to earth will rise again. How long? Not long, because no lie can live forever. . . . How long? Not long, because mine eyes have seen the glory of the coming of the Lord! . . ."

That night, a white housewife from Detroit, Viola Liuzzo, a mother of five, was driving a young black SCLC worker back to Selma when they were ambushed by a car of four Klansmen. Mrs. Liuzzo was killed by a gunshot to the head. The Selma campaign had now taken three lives, though, despite his certain expectations, not King's.

And a few months later, the Voting Rights Act was passed, with provisions for federal supervision of compliance in voter registration, which was to politically transmogrify the South beyond anything that could have been imagined during the Montgomery bus boycott just nine years earlier.

The truth was, even King's victorious campaigns like Selma and Birmingham were not to leave immediate, significantly improved conditions in those communities where they took place, and many local black citizens and civil rights workers would feel that King had only "come and gone," as one complained, like a mere passing gale — that in short they had been used. And in a sense, they had been — as the setting for confrontations to produce national effects, the Public Accommodations Law, the Voting

Rights Act, that would ultimately transform life for blacks in those locales and everywhere else as well. To appreciate just how much, one need only consider how profoundly the South was re-created after King's movement.

Indeed, to anyone newly looking around the South some fifteen years later, it would seem a whole century had passed. The integration of its public life — in restaurants, stores, schools, sports, theaters — had become not only pervasive but commonplace, with a calm ordinariness, almost an unnoticeability, in itself a kind of wonder. In the same way, the prospect of blacks in authority in its civil life had passed from a matter of the unthinkable to a matter of course. In many of its counties now were black sheriffs, and black mayors in its towns and cities, including eventually even Birmingham. By 1980, its legislatures held more black representatives, proportionately, than most other states in the Union. Correspondingly, with the exponential boom in black voter registration, the South's old carbuncular segregationists like Strom Thurmond had begun displaying the most extraordinary solicitudes for the African American populations in their states. And of all these spectacles of the South's political metamorphosis, perhaps none had more an air of historical hallucination than those involving George Wallace, especially after his crippling in an assassination attempt in 1972 — his midfield crowning of a black homecoming queen at the University of Alabama ten years after his doorway stand there, his exuberant appearance at a convocation of black Alabama mayors, grabbing hands with an eager conviviality, including a buss on the cheek of the white wife of the Tuskegee mayor.

At the least, it left one with the suspicion of how ephemeral, after all, might be the old human furies of intransigence and irreconcilability. And it prompted a speculation as well that it might just be the South, which had long served as the theater for the whole country's periodic struggles to exorcise its aboriginal crime of slavery, where America's abiding racial schism might first find resolution. It seemed, however still tentative and uneven, a beginning realization of the original Blessed Community dream of King's movement, a phenomenon unimaginable without the nonviolent spirit of that movement.

Even so, while the South's transformation brought to whites the beginning of a liberation from the fears of the generations before them, it had hardly dispelled as yet the effects on blacks of three centuries of psychic conditioning as a subject people — or the economic disparities that continued to resist the political revolution there. In the end, King's movement did not deliver the blacks of the South full into Canaanland. But it had opened up that land to them.

But King's victory in Selma effectively constituted the end, the benediction, to the classic Southern phase of his movement. All along, his perspectives about the state of American society at large had been waxing more radical, and now Stanley Levison — his old friend and co-visionary from the Montgomery days — advised him that "the elements who responded were for the first time a true cross-section of America," which had left King, Levison stressed, *one of the most powerful figures in the country — a leader now not merely of Negroes, but of millions of whites.*" This, while King himself remained without "obligations to any political party or other dominant interests. Seldom has anyone in America come up by this path." And he now led "one of the rare *independent* movements," Levison told King, which was "the single movement in the nation at this time which arouses the finer democratic instincts of the nation." It had become nothing less than "the great moral force in the country today."

To be sure, King had already begun to expand his social apostleship beyond the South to what, as Andrew Young described it, "has now emerged as a total fight for economic justice and world peace." For that matter, as early as the Kennedy administration's Bay of Pigs exploit, King had declared, "For some reason, we just don't understand the meaning of the revolution taking part in the world . . . against colonialism, reactionary dictatorship, and systems of exploitation." Then, during the Selma campaign, King, in an address at Howard University, had decried for the first time in public the war in Vietnam, calling for a negotiated settlement to end the metastasizing violence there, "which is accomplishing nothing." Such sentiments seemed to many unsettling enough, but more, King propounded in one memo to his SCLC associates that within the United States itself "we are engaged in a social revolution . . . to bring about certain basic structural changes in the architecture of American society." Already there had begun the flash combustions of rage in Malcolm's ghettos in the large cities beyond the South, and when, the very summer after Selma, the Los Angeles section of Watts exploded in riots and burnings, King was left after a visit there "absolutely undone," in the words of Bayard Rustin. King termed it afterward "a class revolt of the underprivileged against privilege" and confessed that he recognized that while the movement had made progress "in the middle classes, the masses remain the same." Right after Selma, then, some in the SCLC — particularly Bevel and their newest enlistee, Jesse Jackson — began beseeching King to open up a new front in the North, in Chicago, and King finally could not resist agreeing.

In fact, he was already evidencing that vastly larger restlessness that would culminate in the last great exertion of his life, the Poor People's Campaign, announcing that "social peace must spring from economic justice" and proposing "a massive assault upon slums, inferior education, inadequate medical care . . . the entire culture of poverty," to redress at last the past systemic economic depredations of both blacks and whites. He had been astonished by statistics presented him by a staffer showing that most of the nation's poor were actually white, and he was soon decreeing that the movement must bend more to the deliverance too "of the so-called poor white."

This larger social mission had always been implicit in King's vision and should not have surprised anyone listening closely to his message over the years, even his comment in Norway during the Nobel Prize visit that America had "much to learn from Scandinavia's democratic socialist tradition" and "the manner in which you have overcome many of the social and economic problems that plague a far more powerful and affluent nation." But in this ultimate ambition now, King would be moving into a stage of struggle where the Gandhian equation of the moral power of popular mass protest against the ruling interests applied even less than in the South: in this case, there was no larger constituency of conscience and governmental concern to appeal to for intercession — it would be true civil conflict. Levison also warned King about the perils of this far larger territory into which he was embarking. Such an extension was almost certain to seriously jostle the coalition of sympathizers — the Northern liberal establishment, its representatives in Washington — on which the Southern movement for the emancipation of blacks there had critically depended. That coalition, Levison cautioned, was still "basically a coalition for moderate change . . . without excessive upheavals," and more than that, "America today is not ready for a radical restructuring of its economy and social order." If King was now to take the movement in the direction of such a hope, it "can head into a cul-de-sac."

Yet King was to cast himself against all this anyway. He may have arrived with Birmingham and Selma at his apotheosis as the Mosaic figure leading his people out of the old Egypt of their bondage in the South, but with this grander aspiration "to confront the power structure massively" on a national scale, he was entering full into his tragic arc.

The Far Country

So King moved out in the months after Selma to undertake a "moral reconstruction" of all American society like that he had worked in the South — and the first battleground of that immensely enlarged struggle was to be Chicago.

In a way the most American of the nation's major cities, bulking big and blusterous in the upper heart of the country, Chicago also happened to be not infrequently referred to as "the Birmingham of the North" — a monolith of unofficial, extrastatutory, but nonetheless strictly separate racial containment. Almost a third of its population of 3.5 million were black, about half of those living in hard poverty, most of them in the Dostoyevskian slums on the city's South and West Sides. In the summer of 1965, riots had flared not only there and in Watts, but in other cities outside the South, Philadelphia, Jersey City, Rochester, the gains by the movement having excited expectations everywhere that were now leapfrogging beyond those advances, especially in the ghettos outstripping any immediate likelihood of fulfillment. With this developing national crisis, King declared, it had taken on the proportions of an emergency "to instill the philosophy of nonviolence in the North"; as Andrew Young put it, "We have got to deliver results — nonviolent results in a Northern city — to protect the nonviolent movement." Failure to do that in Chicago would likely mean the relegation of King's movement to only a parochial, Southern, dated relevance and thus its effective nullification as the one popular force with any possibility for coping with the angers of the black urban masses. But King proposed, "If we can break the system in Chicago, it can be broken anywhere in the country."

A coalition of local civil rights activists that had already formed there combined now with the SCLC for what was called the Chicago Freedom Movement, announced by King as a campaign "to bring about the unconditional surrender of those forces dedicated to the creation and maintenance of slums." With most whites blithely oblivious to how "depressed living standards for Negroes are a structural part of the economy," King asserted, the Chicago Freedom Movement would mount "massive action," as it was described in an SCLC working paper, to "reveal the agents of exploitation and paint a portrait of the evils which beset us in such a manner that it is clear the world over," and "create the kind of coalition of conscience which is necessary to produce change in the country."

That, of course, had always been the operational moral equation of King's movement in the South, but from the start of the Chicago enterprise, there were uncertainties about just how successfully that movement could survive the shift from the spiritual warmth of its Southern genesis into the different climes of the urban North. Bevel argued, "The real estate dealers in Chicago are the equivalent to Wallace and Jim Clark in the South," and that "you don't even have to philosophize about housing in Chicago, you can show that on television." Even so, King seemed to anticipate that matters would not be quite so plain in this effort: instead of any particular antagonist or egregious episodes of abuse, they would be "fighting the system" that had produced an interior Third World society of slums in America as "little more than a domestic colony which leaves its inhabitants dominated politically, exploited economically."

But in all this ambitious language about addressing "the system" lurked precisely the problem. In places like Birmingham and Selma, it was possible to present "a simplification of the issue," the SCLC working paper conceded, "to the point where every citizen of good will, black and white, could respond and identify." But the pattern of racism that permeated life in Chicago and the rest of the country, in jobs and housing and education, persisted apart from any overtly racist laws as in the South, no less profound for being more a disembodied system of custom and attitudes, but that making it far more elusive to engage — it was instead like some vague, malign smog.

King acknowledged that "deep prejudices and discriminations exist in hidden and subtle and covert disguises" in the North, and the "eradication of slums housing millions is complex far beyond integrating buses and lunch counters." Against this, the Chicago Movement would mobilize slum tenants into "unions" to employ rent strikes against intransigent landlords and indifferent city housing officials, as well as multitudinous nonviolent demonstrations.

The larger purposes in these popular actions included demands that the city's housing authority commit to rehabilitating its low-cost public housing and constructing new residential units within and without the slum areas; that lending institutions, real estate agents, business and labor executives, urban renewal authorities, and the city's government all publicly bind themselves irrevocably to policies for the dissolution of slums in Chicago. But in this undertaking, King was confronting a firmament of power and interests, a nebulous field of resistance, lacking the simple fevered palpability of a Wallace or Bull Connor. "His great strength in the old fight was his ability to dramatize the immorality he opposed," wrote David Halberstam, but in Chicago, it was finally "an immorality with invisible sources."

Beyond that, he was attempting to transfer the preacherly inspirations of his movement in the South to blacks in the North, who "were more angry than afraid," as Bevel himself recognized. Once in Chicago, when a riot began developing after police had peremptorily shut off a fire hydrant opened by youths to cool themselves in the midsummer heat, King's efforts to calm the unrest were received not with the reverential deference of blacks in Mississippi or Alabama, but with an outcry of taunts and disdain that King, for the first time, as Abernathy later reported, "could neither reason with nor overpower with his rhetoric." Whatever King's concord with most of Chicago's black leadership, his communion with its slum population remained always tenuous. The difficulty was, he explained once, "You just can't communicate with the ghetto dweller and at the same time not frighten many whites to death" — a difference that portended even less potential rapport for racial community than in the South.

Finally, King's extension into Chicago had to contend with the Florentine wiles of its mayor, Richard Daley, who, with the compact figure of a thick-packed cigar, ruled the city with a juggernaut political machine of patronage and sheer organizational brawn that, closely interlocking with the national Democratic Party, was a far more sizable and elaborate power complex than anything King had yet encountered. And Daley himself was to prove altogether too canny to supply King's Chicago venture with the sensational spectacles of resistance by open force frequent in the South.

Initially, Daley had striven mightily through his deputies in the black community to undo support for King's expedition into Chicago, but when it became inevitable, he wired King before his arrival to

259

cordially suggest a personal meeting, indicating that he would find the city's civil rights situation far more cheerful than he might suppose. Affecting then a public readiness to welcome King to town, Daley proclaimed that "all of us are for the elimination of slums" — and shortly announced a new city initiative to accomplish just that by the end of the next year. As a start, after King let it be known that he would be installing himself in an apartment in one slum tenement, a brigade of painters, carpenters, plasterers, and electricians descended on the site and rapidly refurbished the entire premises, prompting a local press waggery that King could rescue all Chicago's slums simply by moving from building to building.

However, at one early negotiating session with King and a delegation of movement leaders, Daley sturdily refused to address any of their specific proposals for more comprehensive, systemic reforms. Afterward, he protested to the press that King's people had no real answers themselves to the problems they were raising, which the city was already laboring anyway to ameliorate — and proceeded then to announce more antipoverty measures of his own, while distributing grants and subsidies throughout the black community. One seasoned Chicago civil rights partisan, Robert Lucas, would later reflect, "When it was a battle cry to end the slums, the rats and roaches and all that, Daley agreed to that, oh, yeah. Daley sent out all his inspectors and poisoned rats left and right. Then held press conferences. So Daley took that one away from us." With these nimble appearances of cooperation by Daley, Andrew Young was finally driven to openly admit, "The trouble here is that there has been no confrontation" of the kind in the South "where they interrupted the network programs." After several static months, on into the summer of 1966, during which Daley's ploys had managed to deflect any distinct achievements by the movement, King accused him of attempting "to play tricks with us," and in a warning that, under the circumstances, sounded as much like a plea, he declared that Daley "fails to understand that if gains are not made, and made in a hurry," it would "open the door to militant groups to gain a foothold." Demonstrations would have to escalate now, he said, which, while remaining nonviolent, would produce greater dislocations in the accustomed everyday life of the city — but "which would you prefer," King appealed, "this or a riot?"

Riots did soon develop, but of another complexion. Thwarted so far in their "war on slums" by Daley's preemptive maneuvering, "that's when we decided," Lucas would recount, "to march into white neighborhoods for open housing. Because there was no way he was gonna co-opt *that* away from us." The movement's demands already included an end to discrimination in real estate sales; that banks must similarly end racial distinctions in granting mortgage loans; and that the city must seriously enforce its already existing open housing ordinance, making it applicable to owners as well as brokers. With the Chicago Movement shifting to these attentions, King advised that "the reality of equality will require extensive adjustments in the way of life of the white majority." But in challenging Chicago's racially closed residential areas, King was throwing himself against perhaps the most intractable front of American apartheid, one he had never braved in the South — its measureless configuration of segregated neighborhoods, which acted to fracture the whole national community by projecting their racial separations like proliferating fault lines into schools, employment, throughout all economic and social classes in the rest of American society. And it remained the country's most implacable racial fissuring precisely because it was closest to the personal lives of white Americans.

Subsequent open housing marches forging into the tidy streets of Chicago's white neighborhoods — the residential enclaves of the city's ethnic montage of Poles, Lithuanians, Germans, Irish, Italians — were greeted with fusillades of bricks and bottles from mobs howling, "You monkeys! . . . Kill 'em! . . . White power!" Jesse Jackson was hit in the face by a cement block, parked cars of marchers and their leaders were overturned and burned. King himself was once hit by a rock on his temple, sinking to his knees with his head bowed for a moment. Afterward, he told the press that in all his marches in the South, "I have never seen so much hatred and hostility on the faces of so many people . . . as I've seen here today." He had in fact come up against the innermost reality of racism in America.

In a rally then one hot night in a church on the city's West Side, Jackson abruptly announced, after consulting only the movement of his own spirit, a march into Chicago's particularly truculent white suburb of Cicero. As for the wholesale havoc that would almost surely incite, he merely allowed to the press, "We expect violence." Jackson's impromptu wildcat declaration left the SCLC leadership "in trauma," recalls one local movement worker then, but they also had no choice but to commit to the march. "We're not only going to walk in Cicero, we're going to work there and live there," King affirmed. As it turned out, though, the march into Cicero never had to take place: simply the horrendous prospect of it was enough to finally flush from Daley an offer for substantive negotiations.

Two sessions followed between movement leaders and Chicago's political and financial custodians. In the first, Daley, after reading aloud the whole roster of the movement's demands, summarily declared to the astonishment of King and his people that the city would agree to each one — and through that session and the next one, he bluffly shouldered the other members of Chicago's civic establishment, the bankers, the real estate representatives, into giving their consent as well. Afterward, an ebullient King advertised this "Summit Agreement" as holding "far-reaching and creative commitments" to open housing that constituted "the most significant program ever conceived," that "the total eradication of housing discrimination has been made possible." Consequently, King said, the movement would "halt neighborhood marches and demonstrations in Chicago on the issue of open housing, so long as these pledged programs are being carried out."

But before long, the settlement receded into merely an artificial contrivance by the city of a simple profession of agreeable intentions that happened to carry no timetable — but which had nevertheless allowed King to conclude his Chicago enterprise with some semblance of achievement. "It said *nothing*," Lucas was still fretting some thirty years later. "No way to enforce, no teeth in it. *Nothing.*" Commentary in respected press journals deplored this outcome of King's long campaign in Chicago as "only a paper victory," testimonial that "so far, King has been pretty much of a failure at organizing." King himself would later confess to aides that "more specifics should have been included in what was agreed to" and publicly complained that "city agencies have been inert in upholding their commitment to the open housing pact," threatening a resumption of demonstrations. Actually, he and some of his defenders were to contend after Chicago that the agreement there was no more indefinite in particulars than the Birmingham settlement, and the final responsibility for forcing such accords into reality had to pass to the local movement. Some in the Chicago movement, though, protested that the black community felt "sold out"; one wrote King that the settlement had been a "shattering event," leaving only "bewilderment and confusion," a sense of having been "betrayed." As months passed with little detectable evidence of any compliance with the agreement, continuing skirmishes by local activists managed only negligible effects. Things in the city — the isolation and squalor of the slums, the inviolate sanctums of the white neighborhoods — abided more or less as they always had. "There's no question," Lucas would declare, "King was beaten here." And it had largely come about, incredibly, from much the same sort of sleight of hand, the mummery of a supposed agreement, that had confounded him in Albany.

Abernathy would recall Chicago as "an embittering experience, and I'm not sure Martin ever got over it." In fact, he confided to several journalists that Chicago had confirmed for him the endemic, infinitely resourceful intransigence of racism throughout all American society. Already in California, voters had overwhelmingly approved an initiative, Proposition 14, retracting all open housing laws in the state; and from his defiant doorway pose to prevent the integration of the University of Alabama, George Wallace had romped on into a presidential candidacy that came astonishingly close to winning primaries in Wisconsin, Indiana, and Maryland — in the process disclosing the vast submerged continent of white racial resentment in the nation. After Cleveland's Hough ghetto detonated in flames in the summer of 1966, in 1967 there were riots in twenty-three cities, including maelstroms in Newark and Detroit. These ultimately produced the Kerner Commission Report on Civil Disorders, with its famous finding attributing those inner-city eruptions largely to a systemic white racism that was dividing America irrevocably into "two societies . . . separate and unequal."

King, too, himself had declared at an anniversary commemoration of the battle of Birmingham, "White America never did intend to integrate housing, integrate schools, or be fair with the Negro about jobs." He began holding forth that "we are now embarked upon a radical refurbishing of the former racist caste order of America," declaring in one speech, "Freedom is never voluntarily granted by the oppressor. It must be demanded by the oppressed." Altogether, the defeat in Chicago had conducted King, as David Halberstam observed around that time, "closer to Malcolm than anyone would have predicted five years ago — and much further from more traditional allies. . . ."

II

Even before the finish of his Chicago effort, many were already proposing that history had swept beyond King, the movement passing from a moral struggle to one of mere power conflict. By this perspective, the exhaustion of King's nonviolent crusade had been signaled by the emergence in 1965, out in the spectral, moss-ragged countryside of Alabama's Lowndes County, of the Black Panther protest party — the politically insurrectionary handiwork of SNCC and Stokely Carmichael, the long lean black Robespierre who had finally dislodged the gentler-spirited John Lewis as its chairman. "I'm not gonna beg the white man for anything I deserve," Carmichael bugled forth, "I'm gonna *take it!*" Romanticism about the movement in the liberal salons of the North had begun shifting to its incendiaries like

Carmichael, with their terminal cynicism about the efficacy of the ethic of nonviolence, their Malcolm mentality of a final, bitter acceptance of the human condition as one of hopeless racial antagonism. What seemed to be happening everywhere around King, in fact, was something like the tidal ebbing of faith in Matthew Arnold's *Dover Beach*: a withdrawal to naked shingles of anger. And those inheriting that barrenness were the quick, hot, existential revolutionaries like SNCC, with a visceral aversion to any serious intercourse with establishment interests, believing in nothing so much as simple pure action, evincing a certain will to the anarchic.

In the midst of King's Chicago campaign, James Meredith — the first black admitted to the University of Mississippi after federal force subdued a nightlong riot there, who had remained a peculiarly detached, self-enclosed, somewhat erratic personality — made the lone decision to set out on a personal march from Memphis to Jackson, Mississippi, as a one-man demonstration of defiance of the state's rule of terror, he said, to brace the spirit of its black populace. When he was wounded in a shotgun ambush on the second day of his walk, movement leaders, including King and

Carmichael, resolved to continue the march for him and proceeded along the highway under a testily impatient attendance by Mississippi state troopers and the occasional perusal, easing back and forth past them in his pickup truck, of Byron De La Beckwith, as yet unconvicted for the murder of Medgar Evers. Once, as the troopers were shoving marchers off the pavement to the side of the road, Carmichael was restrained from leaping at one of them only by King's firmly unyielding interlocked arm.

But in the voter registration rallies in communities along the way that accompanied their progress, Carmichael's SNCC contingent began chorusing, instead of "We Shall Overcome," *We shall overrun . . .* along with *Jingle bells, shotgun shells, freedom all the way. Oh, what fun it is to blast a trooperman away! . . .* Finally, at a large nighttime rally in Greenwood, Carmichael, his rhetoric whirling like bonfire sparks up into the dark sky, echoed Malcolm's call for blacks to take their political and economic destiny into their own hands and raised the cry, "We want Black Power! We want Black Power!" — an incantation that again rose beating around King when he appeared at the next evening's rally there.

King quickly sensed that "Black Power"

was a shout — the full assertion now of that distemper building at least since Albany — that would be besieging him from this point on. He continued on to a mass meeting in Yazoo City, where he appealed that nothing could be more profitless and suicidal than for blacks to be beguiled into turning to the folly of Black Power against the white majority: "There's going to have to be a coalition of conscience, and we aren't going to be free here in Mississippi and anywhere else in the United States until there is a committed empathy on the part of the white man." For that reason, he declared, "I'm interested in a power that is moral, that is right and good. . . ." But he was stunned by a jeering from many in the sanctuary, and as he would later relate, he lay unable to sleep that night, first with a rankling indignation and then with the pained recognition that, because ever since Montgomery "I had preached to them about my dream," he had been answered that evening with "booing because they felt we were unable to deliver on our promises."

Carmichael later told him, "Martin, I deliberately decided to raise this issue on the march in order to give it a national forum and force you to take a stand. . . ." King gave him one of his regretful little understanding smiles: "I have been used before. One more time won't hurt." In fact, Carmichael had set a tension into play for King not unlike that service Malcolm had promised Coretta in Selma: of presenting to whites the traumatic alternative to King's appeal. As King began telling interviewers, "I'm trying desperately to keep the movement nonviolent, but I can't keep it nonviolent by myself. Much of the responsibility is on the white power structure to give meaningful concessions to Negroes." But one journalist who had long been covering King noted that the outbreak of the Black Power countermovement had left him "physically and emotionally shaken." "I don't know what I'm going to do," King confided to the reporter. Surrender to the abyss sometimes tempted: King once suggested to Abernathy, "Why don't we just step back and let the violent forces run their course? They don't know what they're doing, and it won't last long."

But even while he persisted in decrying Black Power as a "nihilistic philosophy born out of the conviction that the Negro can't win," King worried to one reporter, "Somewhere there has to be a synthesis. I have to be militant enough to satisfy the militant, yet I have to keep enough discipline in the movement to satisfy white supporters and moderate Negroes." He speculated for a while that perhaps the role left to him now was to try to mediate across the deepening racial chasm in the country: "There must be somebody to communicate to the two worlds." Because, he stressed to one audience, it was still the inescapable imperative that in "seeking the profound changes full integration will involve, Negroes need the continued support of the white majority." And against all the indications around him of a dying of faith in his nonviolent vision, he was still insisting, "When I talk about power and the need for power, I'm talking in terms of the need for power to bring about . . . the creation of the Beloved Community."

But as he labored to negotiate that old aspiration through the advent now of Black Power, even journals supportive in the past, like *The Nation*, were maintaining that King's movement was nearing its end. To his passionate oratories, black urban youths, one newsman noticed, only "laughed or simply ignored him and began talking among themselves" — there had arisen a generation to whom he could no longer connect, who did not know him. Andrew Kopkind in the *New York Review of Books* declared, "He has been outstripped by his times, overtaken by the events which he may have obliquely helped to produce but would not predict," and although some still contended that with his " 'nobility' and the purity of his humanism . . . the world is not ready for him," it was more the case that "King is not ready for the world."

Nevertheless, King kept resolutely proclaiming that "even if every Negro in the United States comes to think that Negroes ought to riot," that "if every Negro in the United States turns to violence, I will choose to be that one lone voice preaching that this is the wrong way." To a mass meeting in Mississippi, he cried out, "I'm sick and tired of violence. I'm tired of the war in Vietnam. I'm tired of war and conflict in the world. I'm tired of shooting. I'm tired of hatred. I'm tired of selfishness. I'm tired of evil." But "I'm not going to use violence, no matter who says it."

At the same time, even as his own public stature seemed steadily diminishing, he was drawn ineluctably into an apostleship against the nation's magnifying military adventure in Vietnam, during a period still of general popular favor for that exploit — announcing that simply as a minister of Jesus' gospel "I am mandated by this calling above every other duty to seek peace among men and to do it even in the face of hysteria and scorn." As the expense of sustaining the escalating operations in Vietnam began to consume Johnson's ambitions for a War on Poverty and the Great Society, King called it only another illustration of how wrong abroad and wrong at home were "inextricably bound together." "The bombs in Vietnam explode at home," he declared. "They destroy the dreams and possibilities for a decent America." Besides, he warned, "It's worthless to talk about integrating if there is no world to integrate."

But King's aide Bernard Lee would later tell biographer David Garrow that King decided to fully commit himself to opposing the war only when he was ruffling through several magazines in an airport restaurant and suddenly stopped at a photo spread in *Ramparts* of Vietnamese children burned in U.S. napalm attacks. "He froze. . . . He saw a picture of a Vietnamese mother holding her dead baby" and then pushed his plate of food away, Lee recounted. "I said, 'Doesn't it taste any good?' and he answered, 'Nothing will ever taste any good for me until I do everything to end that war.' " From that point on, Vietnam became an obsession with King, impelling him at times into rhetoric that discomfited even close aides; once he bayed out to an antiwar rally in Chicago that America was "standing before the world glutted by our own barbarity."

He delivered what he intended to be his major pronouncement on Vietnam at New York's Riverside Church in the spring of 1967. The war, he declared, was being waged on behalf of "the wealthy and secure while we create a hell for the poor," devastating any prospects for alleviating their destitution at home, conscripting them instead to be killed in that unholy conflict abroad. He demanded the United States halt all bombing, commit to a unilateral cease-fire, agree to the inclusion of the Vietcong in peace talks, and set a deadline for the withdrawal of its troops. He also urged all youths when drafted to declare themselves conscientious objectors. As a gospel preacher, he had to testify out of "allegiances and loyalties that are broader and deeper than nationalism," he intoned, and "I know that I could never again raise my voice against the violence of the oppressed in the ghettos without having first spoken clearly to the greatest purveyor of violence in the world today — my own government." In the end, he propounded, "the war in Vietnam is but a symptom of a far deeper malady within the

American spirit," and it held the direst implications for the country's future: "If we are to get on the right side of the world revolution, we as a nation must undergo a radical revolution of values. We must rapidly begin the shift from a thing-oriented society to a people-oriented society."

Earlier, when King had confided to Stanley Levison that he had concluded he must make a definitive, open break with Johnson by campaigning full-tilt against the war, Levison had cautioned that he could "become identified as the leader of a fringe movement" and that it could financially wreck an already precariously funded SCLC. King knew, he conceded, that "I will get a lot of criticism and I know it can hurt SCLC," but "I feel so deep in my heart that we are wrong in this country and the time has come for a real prophecy, and I'm willing to go that road."

King was indeed passing now into that far country of all true prophets ultimately: that lonely region beyond the conventionally enlightened, the standard civic respectability, where he was to enjoy far less company than during the Washington and Selma Marches. With the wide support for the war at that time, his outcry against it not only earned him the instant rancor of Lyndon Johnson's

Washington, but outraged such usual sympathizers in the past as *The New York Times*, which, after his Riverside Church speech, deplored his effort to muddle the civil rights movement with agitation against the war and "recklessly comparing American military methods to those of the Nazis." *The Washington Post* deemed it "a great tragedy" that he should be inflicting such "a grave injury to those who are his natural allies [and] an even graver injury to himself. Many who have listened to him with respect will never again accord him the same confidence." Henry Luce's *Life* flatly termed his Riverside Church address "a demagogic slander that sounded like a script for Radio Hanoi." In all, King found himself the subject of the polemical equivalent of a crowd mugging.

J. Edgar Hoover did not lose this chance to exhort Johnson in a private memo: "Based on King's recent activities and public utterances, it is clear that he is an instrument in the hands of subversive forces seeking to undermine our nation." In fact, communications between King and the White House had already ceased, owing not only to Johnson's towering umbrage at King's protests of the war, but to King's own virtual nausea of disappointment with what he saw now as a deformity of character in

Johnson. But his evangelism against the war distressed even many in his traditional constituency in the black community: to King's professed hope to "combine the civil rights movement with the peace movement," the prestigious Ralph Bunche — black U.S. delegate to the United Nations and winner himself of the Nobel Peace Prize in 1950, who had been among those walking beside King in the Selma March — voiced alarm about this dubious amalgamation of the movement with war protests, averring King should "give up one or the other."

The NAACP's Roy Wilkins and Urban League director Whitney Young also publicly disassociated themselves from King's Vietnam preachments, and at a private reception on Long Island, there transpired a brief clash between Young and King — Young coming over to upbraid King for anti-Vietnam statements that could chill Johnson toward all the movement's leadership. King flared, "Whitney, what you're saying may get you a foundation grant, but it won't get you into the kingdom of truth." Young gave King a swift up-and-down glare and, mentioning King's campaign against urban poverty, motioned at his plump midriff and retorted, "You're eating well." With heads now turning toward them, a mutual friend intervened to pull King aside before the altercation could develop further. But within the SCLC itself, there was no little unease about King's fixation on Vietnam; one board member, Aaron Henry of Mississippi's COFO summer, later recalled, "It appeared to me that we were taking a position here that we had really no knowledge of exactly what we were doing." To such admonitions, King admitted he was not that thoroughly versed in all the considerations forming the administration's Vietnam policy, but "I *am* expert in recognition of a simple eloquent truth. That truth is that it is sinful for any of God's children to brutalize any of God's other children. . . ."

Even so, King himself seemed to recoil now and then from the consequences of this new witness of his. Polls disclosed a huge popular disapproval of his antiwar ministry, including substantial discontent (48 percent) in the black community. "We have to face the fact that sometimes the public is not ready to digest the truth," he offered to his staff, but he acknowledged that his "star is waning" because of Vietnam. "They have all the news media and TV," he despaired to close aides, "and I just don't have the strength to fight all these things *and* keep my civil rights fight going. . . . I'm already overloaded and almost emotionally fatigued." Although he had felt compelled to raise "a question that deals with the survival of mankind," with the furor it had provoked perhaps he should "gracefully pull out" for a while and return to his civil rights mission, because "I can't battle these forces who are out . . . to cut me down." One evening after an SCLC conference in Virginia, he brooded to Joan Baez after downing a number of drinks, she later recounted, "that the Lord had called him to be a preacher, and not to do all this stuff, and he wanted to leave it and he was tired. . . ."

Actually, the backfire had become so wide and vituperative that King had several times collapsed into weeping. He declared to one audience in Los Angeles, in what seemed as much a testimonial to the state of his own spirit now, that it was "midnight in our world today. We are experiencing a darkness so deep . . . that we can hardly see which way to turn." In one of those sermons at Ebenezer that were more like compulsive personal confessionals to his congregation, he told them that "we stumble through life with a feeling of insecurity, a lack of self-confidence, and a sense of impending failure. A fear of what life may bring." He kept insisting through this time, "I can't lose hope. I can't lose hope because when you lose hope, you die," but those around King again grew deeply concerned about the shadow closing over his spirit. Coretta would remember that he seemed caught, sluggish and passive, in the thrall of a depression "greater than I had ever seen before." To her worried queries, he would mutter, "People expect me to have answers and I don't have any answers." He was smoking, however furtively, incessantly now. He was eating more heavily, heedlessly, of the soul fare of his boyhood — the fried chicken and fatback-simmered green beans and sweet-potato casseroles savored from that distant Eden of his innocent beginnings.

"I am tired of demonstrating," he blurted openly more than once, "I am tired of the threat of death. I want to live. I don't want to be a martyr. And there are moments when I doubt if I am going to make it through. . . . I don't march because I want to. I march because I must." With a noticeable frequency, he began delivering himself of such public contemplations as, "To be a Christian, one must take up his cross, with all its difficulties and agonizing and tension-packed content, and carry it until that very cross leaves its mark upon us and redeems us to that more excellent way which comes only through suffering." Indeed, looking back now, it is impossible to avoid the analogy that King had entered into a time that was for him like a protracted, precrucifixion ordeal of trial and scourging — a sense obviously as unavoidable for King himself during those days. "When I took up the cross, I recognized its meaning," he told an SCLC retreat. "The cross is something that you bear and ultimately that you die on. . . . And that's the way I have decided to go."

"The difference that I saw over the years," Andrew Young would later reflect, was that from a figure initially uncertain and reluctant and even apprehensive, as in Montgomery, about taking on himself the full weight of responsibility for the movement's future, "he went almost to the other extreme and felt totally responsible and burdened by the movement," to the extent that "Martin felt terribly guilty" for all its adversities now. "He felt he should be able to convince Johnson to withdraw from Vietnam. He felt he should be able to wipe out poverty. He should be able to stop violence." He had in fact now given himself wholly over to, as he sometimes cast it, the struggle against the "isness" of the world by the "eternal oughtness." He belled out one Sunday to his Ebenezer congregation, to a pulsing of answering cries and clapping:

I choose to identify with the underprivileged. I choose to identify with the poor. I
choose to give my life for the hungry. I
choose to give my life for those who have
been left out. . . . This is the way I'm going.
If it means suffering a little bit, I'm going
that way. . . . If it means dying for them, I'm
going that way.

III

But nothing promised to arrest King's
steady waning now in national regard, ob-
servations having become commonplace
that Black Power and the uproar over his antiwar message had thrown him "into great
confusion and doubt," with his ministry
"groping for something it never finds." In
fact, King was moving through a general
season of disillusionment in the nation.
After the strains and tumults of the great social initiatives of the past decade, there had
set in something like a brackish backwash of
popular mood, a weariness of spirit and conscience, and, with the movement having
begun to be assimilated into the turbulence

of the student countercultural revolt, a wider lust for order again — all of which would eventually produce the presidency of Richard Nixon and, after the aberration of Carter, reach its culmination in the warmly affable, autocratic reign of Ronald Reagan.

By 1967 King had come to feel an unease of soul that he was trapped in some accelerating contest between the last hopes for a true, interconnected human community in America and the progressive deadening of its heart by the advance of a new sort of technotronic, corporate totalitarianism — a national order of power, composed of the megaconglomerates and the huge machineries of government acting in their interests, that was working a systematic impoverishment of modern man's very humanity, conducting the country ever further into a computerized, materialistic void. His forebodings about this brought him to a radicalization of perspective ranged against, as it were, the very nature and shape of his times. "For years I labored with the idea of reforming the existing institutions of society" through "a little change here and a little change there," he told David Halberstam, but "now I feel quite differently. You have got to have a reconstruction of the entire society, a revolution of values."

He notified the movement's foundation patrons, himself now echoing Malcolm, "We are not interested in being integrated into *this* value structure. Power must be relocated, a radical distribution of power must take place."

At a private SCLC conclave at a retreat on the South Carolina coast, he seemed driven even to discount all that had taken place since Montgomery: all its "legislative and judicial victories" were "at best surface changes." But the movement must now begin "making demands that will cost the nation something," demands involving not only racial but "class issues." Because "something is wrong with the economic system of our nation ... something is wrong with capitalism." As early as 1965, actually, he had advised supporters that the movement would soon be addressing itself to "the profit system" and expanded: "Call it what you may, call it democracy, or call it democratic socialism, but there must be a better distribution of wealth within this country for all God's children." What he was pondering included a multibillion-dollar Marshall Plan to salvage the inner cities, a guaranteed minimum income for all households, a possible nationalization of the more vital public services and industries:

"There comes a time when any system must be reevaluated."

Testifying at a Senate committee hearing, he asserted that "the solution to poverty is to abolish it directly," through a vast endeavor to assure everyone a job and guaranteed annual income. Indeed, despite the loquaciously specious claims of opponents of the policy in years afterward, King also urged a program of affirmative action as one means to begin rectifying the effects on America's black population of generations of dispossession and exclusion, a "compensatory fairness," as preferments had been accorded GIs removed during their military service out of the main course of America's domestic life.

It would all mean "a much harder struggle," King told the Senate committee, for "a restructuring of the architecture of American society" — but he had in fact largely despaired by now of the will or capacity of electoral government for that struggle. His moral expectations had somewhat contracted, if not to the minimal cynicisms of SNCC, more to the measure of an early contemplation of his about Niebuhr: that "the more aggressively one relates the gospel to life, the more sensitively he realizes that the social unit can accommodate only justice, not agape." He informed the SCLC that they must forge "new tactics which do not depend on government good will, but instead serve to compel unwilling authorities to yield to the mandates of justice." And for that, they must move to the higher militancy, though still on Gandhi's nonviolent terms, of massive civil disobedience.

Thus, in the summer of 1967, King announced what would be the most expansively radical adventure of his life: a national movement called the Poor People's Campaign. It would mobilize into one wide popular front not only blacks but all the country's disregarded and outcast — poor whites, Hispanics, Native Americans — in a great Gandhian crusade that would challenge the nation's entire custodial complex, not just its corporate citadels but its central institutions of government, to free the destitute of America from their generational ghettos of hopelessness. And to "place the problem of the poor at the seat of government of the wealthiest nation in the history of mankind," King declared, a Poor People's March would converge on Washington — in caravans, some by mule wagon, from the poorest recesses of the nation, rural and inner city — to set up a makeshift encampment on the Washington Mall, site of the memorable civil rights rally just five years earlier. From that Mall encampment, demonstrators would then lay concerted siege to the chambers of power in the capital with a campaign of "major dislocations" designed to "cripple the operation of an oppressive government," all to force a humanizing reformation of its policies at home and abroad. Their demand, King told his SCLC staff, would be, "Repent, America!" — that demand including an annual $30 billion federal investment to expunge poverty from the land, with a commitment to full employment, a guaranteed annual income, and construction of three hundred thousand units of low-cost housing each year. In all, it would be an endeavor to move "a sick, neurotic nation," King said, "away from at least a level of its sickness." And this time, he promised, they would "go for broke. . . ."

One of his advisers would later recall, "There was an awareness that we were going to confront the economic foundations of the system . . . what the powers of the country will kill you for." One private backer, a Chicago businessman named Cirilo McSween, remembers that after a conference convoked by King at Ebenezer Church to explain this new initiative to a corps of his supporters, several of them were standing outside the church in the warm evening, discussing all that King had arrayed to them through that day's session, and only then did they fully realize "what it was really all about, the total seriousness of the thing. He had done all these other social things, but this was the culmination . . . it was embarking on the financial structure of the country." It was at that moment, says McSween, that for the first time "we understood that Martin Luther King was a revolutionary. This was big business, absolutely radical. And it had become very dangerous." When King came outside and stood chatting with them for several moments — it happened to be the evening of his thirty-eighth birthday — "he was very relaxed. Even though," McSween recalls, he suddenly became aware "he had no protection at all around him."

Yet even in all this, King still had not lost, despite everything, his old faith in the power finally of moral confrontation to move people of conscience, that the Poor People's Campaign could somehow be "powerful enough, dramatic enough, morally appealing enough, so that people of good will . . . begin to put pressure on Congressmen." But what King was essaying now was nothing less than a reordering of the very economic and power arrangements of the nation, the values and terms on which America worked — an altogether different proposition from simply according constitutional rights to Southern blacks. And with his having followed his original moral vision in Montgomery to its ultimate implications, many more than just J. Edgar Hoover now were appalled and uncomprehending. A number of his past liberal allies came to regard him rather as a Baptist preacher who had wandered beyond his depth, and the defections among his supporters through the past year of Black Power and his Vietnam apostleship multiplied precipitously. King bravely allowed to reporters that "I don't think in a social revolution you can always retain the support of the moderates" — but he struggled anyway, desperately, to keep as many with him as he could. He spent one long night travailing with the misgivings of a Manhattan couple who had remained faithful patrons up to now, entreating their support for this last grand undertaking of his while downing one orange juice and vodka after another; he finally departed around dawn, desolated by their refusal.

But even a number of the inner regulars among King's aides were resisting the Poor People's Campaign as far too sweeping and strategically uncertain a commitment. Jesse Jackson argued, "How are we supposed to counter a rejection from the White House and Congress? If we don't get some results, we'll lose face." Young admits, "None of us were particularly excited about the Poor People's Campaign. Bevel wanted to keep on the war in Vietnam. Hosea wanted to build a political base in the South. Everybody had a different agenda." Neither were they especially inspired when King "talked seriously of mounting the kind of campaign that would possibly lead to our being in prison for a year or two . . . and we knew that was the sort of thing he was leading us into." King, though, despite his old dread of being pent in a prison cell, now seemed to Young "almost as if he were looking forward to spending a couple of years in jail," as though that were the only possible refuge now from the ordeal his mission had become.

His moral perspectives, his sense of the realities, which had turned out momentously apt and able for his movement's Southern struggle, began to look overmatched in what he was now more largely taking on. In fact, his Poor People's Campaign was probably, from the start, a hopelessly misbegotten enterprise for the same reason that his Chicago effort miscarried: again, but on a national scale now, he was addressing a force field of interests far more monolithic but also far more elusive to confront than a Bull Connor or George Wallace's troopers on the Selma Bridge — a profusion of resistance in which, in the words of an old gospel song, *You can't find the one to blame / It's too smart to have a name / It's not flesh and blood we fight with / It's powers and principalities. . . .*

Against this, the Poor People's Campaign was assembling only fitfully, already lapsing into logistical and financial dishevelment, with only a fraction of the multitudes needed for the mass confrontation in Washington as yet enlisted. And the persisting dissents from his own staff had not precisely eased King's sense of embattled aloneness, his growing fatalistic gloom. Visitors found him "a profoundly weary and wounded spirit," with "a profound sadness" having settled over him, and a former SCLC staffer in Los Angeles would recall that he kept maintaining "that his time was up," that "he knew they were out to get him." To another close aide, he seemed in almost a trance of "weariness, just weariness of the struggle."

Yet he could get no more than an hour or two of sleep: when they were on the road together, Young recollected, "he'd want to talk all night long." He was soon reeling into such apocalyptic projections as "I don't have any faith in the whites in power" to abide more inner-city disorders without its "leading inevitably to a right-wing takeover and a fascist state," which would "treat us like they did our Japanese brothers and sisters in World War Two. They'll throw us into concentration camps. . . . They'll cordon off the ghetto and issue passes for us to get in and out."

Early in 1968, only a few months before the Poor People's Campaign was scheduled to commence, King and Abernathy retreated to Acapulco for a short vacation, sharing a room as usual, and Abernathy would remember King slept only scrappily, "frightened by what lay ahead." Outside their room "was this balcony projecting right out over the sea atop a high cliff," Abernathy later recounted, "so when you looked down, there didn't seem anything underneath you but waves breaking far below. And I'd wake up early in the mornings, right before daylight, to see him standin' out on the balcony in his pajamas, standin' real still and just listenin' to that sound of those waves breakin' on this huge rock down there that the sea was crashin' against. Then one morning when I woke up, he was standin' out there singin' a favorite hymn of his, 'Rock of Ages' — and I don't mean quietly, but lettin' it really roll out. . . ."

Still, King had not been able to surrender that old sense of a larger self, of "a cosmic campanionship," that lay in living in the higher meaning of the great historical truth animating a movement that could "save the soul of a nation . . . save the whole of mankind." And though he found himself more beleaguered on all sides, and harrowed by private forebodings and sinkings of will, yet strangely — as if in inverse measure to his despair as he watched the preparations for his "last, greatest dream" beginning to falter around him — King's messianic vision seemed only to wheel out farther, reaching beyond the nation to embrace now almost deliriously the world itself. The social crisis in America, he declared, was "inseparable from an international emergency which involves the poor, the dispossessed, the exploited of the whole world. . . ." It was as if, all these years since his boyhood's unbearable pain when death took his grandmother, he had come to feel laden with all the planet's grief — famines, massacres, maraudings of war, the slums not only of Chicago, but of Cairo and Calcutta and Lima — all the earth's cruelty and anguish. Even as the Poor People's Campaign seemed foundering, he had begun appealing for a yet vaster and climactic movement to accomplish a wholly new global community beyond class, tribe, race, nation — "a world unity in which all barriers of caste and color are abolished."

In one of his last addresses to his congregation at Ebenezer, he declared that all he wanted said about him when he died was "for somebody to mention that day that Martin Luther King, Jr., tried to give his life serving others. I'd like somebody to say that day that Martin Luther King, Jr., tried to love somebody . . . that I did try to feed the hungry . . . to clothe the naked . . . that I tried to love and serve humanity."

In those last weeks, King began suffering from migraine headaches as he continued to contend with those on his staff still contesting the soundness of the Poor People's Campaign. He was then entreated by his old colleague in Gandhian nonviolence, James Lawson, now minister of a church in Memphis, to assist in a strike by the city's black sanitation workers over the mayor's refusal to recognize their union. When King decided to accept Lawson's call for intercession as a kind of preliminary exercise for the larger operation ahead, many of his aides were incredulous — it could only be a pointless diversion, too small and incidental, in what was already a colossally dubious project. "We felt like you just couldn't take on everything," says Young, "and if we went into Memphis, we'd get bogged down there and never get to Washington. But Martin said he couldn't turn his back on those garbage workers." In fact, he insisted, it was precisely the sort of situation the Poor People's Campaign was all about.

In an initial exploratory sojourn into Memphis, King led a protest march that swiftly devolved into a riot, store windows shattered, merchandise looted, a number bloodied by thrown rocks. After aides had spirited King away, police suppressed the disorder with salvos of tear gas, and one black youth was fatally shot. Fifty people in all were injured, another 120 arrested, with over 3,000 National Guardsmen called in to enforce a curfew. Back in his motel room, King lay in bed under the covers with all his clothes on, "in a kind of despair," Young later related, "that I had never seen before. A real, deep-seated depression because he felt he was responsible and had miscalculated." He burst out to Abernathy at one point, "Ralph, I want you to get me out of Memphis. Get me out of Memphis as soon as possible." In his exorbitant agonizing over the incident, he considered a penitential fast, telling Stanley Levison that his critics would now be proclaiming that "Martin Luther King is dead, he's finished. His nonviolence is nothing, no one is listening to it. . . . Martin Luther King is at the end of his rope." For that matter, J. Edgar Hoover all this while had been no less tenacious in his pursuit of King, and though he had suspended the wiretaps of King's hotel rooms out of alarm about congressional investigations into the FBI's electronic surveillance operations, his agents were still devising means for sabotaging the Poor People's Campaign, and were now directed to establish the circumstances of King's responsibility for the riot for leaking to receptive newsmen.

Back in Atlanta, King "got very, very quiet," remembers Young, "and spent almost from Monday to Friday alone. Saw almost nobody." He then summoned his inner staff to a meeting in a study at Ebenezer, where he "just jumped on everybody," says Young. "He said we all had let him down . . .

said, 'I can't take all this on myself, I need you to take your share of the load.' " He finally fumed out of the room, and Jackson trailed after him, calling from the top of the stairs as King was turning on the landing below, "Doc? Doc? Don't worry, everything's going to be all right." King swung a finger up at Jackson: "Everything's *not* going to be all right if things keep going the way they're going." Young recalls, "It was shocking in the sense that . . . nobody had ever seen him mad like that before." King then bolted off for the comforting refuge of the apartment of one of his paramours in Atlanta.

That was on a Saturday. Four days later, on Wednesday, April 3, 1968, King and Abernathy returned to Memphis, landing just as a storm was darkly closing over the city. In their room at the Lorraine Motel, King decided Abernathy should speak in his stead at the mass meeting scheduled that evening at Mason Temple. But despite the heavy pounding of rain in the hot night, Abernathy found when he arrived at the church a sizable crowd awaiting King expectantly, along with a battery of network news cameras, and he phoned King at the Lorraine to urge that he come after all.

King shortly appeared, to jubilant cheers

and clapping, for what was to be the last mass meeting of his life. When he took the pulpit, lightning was still flashing outside with claps of thunder. The night was so sweltering that "the fans were on," recalls a local minister in the church that night, the Reverend Samuel Kyles; and as King began speaking, the fans "would bang now and then, and each time they did, King gave a start. So they finally shut them off." King's heavy, measured voice knelled over the congregation, mounting in momentum to the accompanying surges of shouts and applause, in what happened to be much the same message that he had delivered to that church rally in Montgomery some twelve years before: *Well, I don't know what will happen now. We've got some difficult days ahead, but it really doesn't matter with me now —*

because I've been to the mountaintop. And I don't mind. Like anybody, I would like to live a long time, longevity has its place. But I'm not concerned about that now. I just want to do God's will —

And in that familiar way of his oratory at mass meetings from Montgomery on through to Selma, from the same spontaneously massing compressions of passion, he pealed out with a roll of his head and mouth opening wide in an organ-billowing call:

And He's allowed me to go up to the mountain, and I've looked over, and I've *seeeen* the Promised Land!

In the tumult of rejoicing that broke out at this point in the church — as Jesse Jackson, who was there with other King aides, would afterward report — "He was lifted up and had some mysterious aura around him, and a power . . . The crowd was tremendously moved, in tears. . . ." King boomed on:

I may not get there with you. But I want you to know tonight that we, as a people, *will* get to the Promised Land! And so I'm happy tonight! I'm not fearing any man! Mine eyes have seen the glory of the coming of the Lord!

With that finish, to the transported thundering in the church, King appeared to reel back from the pulpit, and Abernathy leapt up to hold him. King's face was shining with sweat, tears in his eyes. But to Abernathy, he seemed restored to his old exaltation.

The two of them then set out with another

King aide, Abernathy was to report only years later, for a late dinner at the home of a woman with whom King had kept company before, and from that point on, according to Abernathy, King flung himself into a final, all-night release into carnal carousal. Around one in the morning, he emerged from a bedroom with the woman, and he and Abernathy returned to the Lorraine, where they found another of King's consorts waiting for them. King disappeared with her until after dawn, and when he returned to the room he and Abernathy were sharing, they saw, by Abernathy's account, yet a third of King's inamoratas leaving the motel, miffed by his other assignation there. King pleaded with Abernathy to bring her back, but after an angry scuffle in the room, she rushed out again, with King crying after her, "Don't go! Don't go!"

Late that afternoon, then — Thursday, April 4 — as King and Abernathy were preparing to leave with other SCLC staffers for a Southern soul food dinner at the home of Reverend Kyles before that evening's mass meeting, Abernathy told him, "Wait a minute, I forgot to put on some aftershave lotion." King stepped out onto the second-floor room's walkway balcony in the soft, warm, spring dusk, still in his shirtsleeves and tucking in his shirttail, and began chatting with a loose and easy joviality with several aides clustered in the parking court below him. He leaned forward with both hands braced on the balcony railing and called down to a saxophonist and soloist, Ben Branch, whom Jackson had brought from Chicago to perform at that night's meeting: "Ben, I want you to sing 'Precious Lord' for me tonight like you never sung it before. Want you to sing it *real* pretty." King's local driver then advised him the evening air seemed turning cool and he should get his topcoat, and King, saying, "Okay, Jonesy," was straightening up to turn back into his room when there racketed over the courtyard, like a startling slap against the calm of that spring twilight, a single loud shot.

Abernathy would relate that, in the bathroom splashing on the aftershave lotion, "I heard this *pop,* like a firecracker, and looked around. All I could see from inside the room were his feet lying out on the balcony, sticking out just beyond the edge of the glass door, you know, and I thought, *Somebody's shootin' up the place,* I thought. *He's lying down like they teach you to do in the service —* but then I heard groans from the people standin' outside in the courtyard, heard hollerin', 'Oh, Lord! Oh, Lord!' And I knew. . . ."

King had been jolted backward to his left, one witness seeing him "go up with the shot against the wall, and as he went up his arms went out to his sides like he was a man on a cross." He lay slumped across the balcony floor with his knees lifted slightly, his shoes crammed awkwardly against the railing slats and trying to move "like riding a bicycle," some observed, his left arm outflung where it had fallen from its instinctive grope for the railing as he toppled. At the shot, the people in the courtyard had thrown themselves to the pavement, and Reverend Kyles and Abernathy were the first to reach King. His neck and right jaw were blasted open, blood brimming into a heavy pool around his shoulders. Abernathy would recount a few weeks later:

I bent over him and yelled, "Martin! Martin! Martin!" I seemed to get his attention, and I patted him on the cheek and said, "Martin, this is Ralph. Don't worry, it's gonna be all right, it's gonna be all right." He tried to say something, his lips tried to move, but all he could do was look at me. It was like he was talking through his eyes — and what they were saying was, *It has come. It has happened.* . . .

In a moment, the balcony was swarming with other people, King's aides, a white official in the Community Relations Service who clumsily swaddled King's head in a towel. Kyles ripped an orange bedspread from the room and brought it out to cover King, removing from King's hand a crushed pack of cigarettes: "King never smoked in public, so I took it out of his hand." Abernathy, Young, and several others accompanied King's body in an ambulance to a hospital, and when they returned to the Lorraine an hour or so later, Abernathy brought out to the balcony a cardboard sheet from a laundered shirt and bent, Young remembers, "scooping the blood into a jar" — weeping as he did, "This is Martin's precious blood. This blood was shed for us." Jesse Jackson then leaned down and placed both hands, palms downward, into the pool of blood, and stood and wiped both hands down the front of his shirt. Young would later explain, "We Baptists, you know, we believe there's a power in the blood — power that's transferable." Historian and journalist Garry Wills later noted, in a commentary about that bizarre scene, that it has immemorially been a deep human urge in such instances of violent martyrdom to dip one's hands into, preserve on oneself some touch of, the blood of a slain prophet and hero.

For all the fallings away of belief that had come to oppress King through the past year, it was yet as if that rifle clap in the April dusk in Memphis split apart the very sky of hope for masses of Americans, setting off conflagrations of fury in inner cities across the nation, smoke even dimming the sun over the white domes of Washington. And over the following weeks, it would come to seem that King's death had been almost a personal enactment of the death of the nonviolent movement in America, extinguished with him the nation's highest moral adventure in recent history. Despite his apparent decline, in that awful definition sometimes of violent annihilation, it suddenly appeared after Memphis that on no one else — save, perhaps, for a brief while, remarkably, Robert Kennedy — had the last possibility for averting a final irreconcilable racial schism in the country so immediately depended. The Poor People's Campaign, mounted in the summer a few weeks after Memphis, became more or less the moment of truth for the continuation of King's movement beyond King. A haphazard agglomeration of plyboard shelters was set up along the Washington Mall to house some two thousand demonstrators, and named Resurrection City. But from the start, the whole effort staggered under the SCLC's simultaneous struggle to reconstruct itself somehow around the void left by King's death. Abernathy, selected at King's earlier behest to succeed him as the SCLC's leader, passed through those weeks after Memphis still in a daze, a displaced and sleepy look in his eyes: while flying about the country trying to salvage both the SCLC and the Poor People's Campaign, he would sit slumped in a front-row seat, a somewhat disreputable-looking curiosity in rumpled, soiled denims among the cabin of businessmen in synthetic suits and wafer-thin briefcases, and in the dull jet roar he would obsessively insist to whatever reporter might be riding with him, "This is just something that's been thrust on me. I didn't ask for it. I didn't kill Martin Luther King."

At one outdoor rally in Philadelphia, Abernathy blared from the platform, "Don't expect me to be Martin Luther King. Nothing's gonna bring him back. A sick America killed him, and now he's gone. But I wanna tell America — you killed him, but now, be dog if you not gonna have your hands full with Ralph Abernathy!" He took heart in the cheers. "Now I ain't a handsome man —" SCLC assistants in the crowd sought to embolden him by yelling, "Oh, yeah, you are, Ralph!" "Naw, I ain't a handsome man. But I'm *all* man" — and he yanked apart his denim shirt, baring to the crowd his chest with its crisping soot of hair — "I ain't but five foot eight, but if that ain't tall enough, I can stand on my tiptoes!" After the rally, as a car bore him through a churn and eddy of people, some of King's old aides riding with him set up a spirited clamoring, "We have a movement! Yes, sir, we have a movement!" But Abernathy merely sat with a heavy inertness in their midst, on his face a lost and muzzy expression, as if he were hearing their effusions from some far distance.

After barely two months, Resurrection City had deteriorated, under steadily battering rains, into much a slum itself, static and isolated in the mud, and at last ended up, taking all the Poor People's Campaign along with it, as probably the first major civil rights offensive to succumb to a minor legal nicety — the expiration of its land use permit. Early one morning, National Guardsmen trampled through the rows of shanties, flushing out the last few shadowy occupants, then swiftly dismantled the whole encampment. So vanished the last and largest dream of King's life.

After that, all that managed to hold his aides together for a short while was the ghost of King; but with the gravity of his actual presence now gone, they soon began to loop off into their separate and widely diverse orbits. Jesse Jackson, after founding his own movement organization in Chicago, would eventually convert what was perhaps the largest victory of King's apostleship — the claiming of the vote for all blacks — into two surprisingly impressive guerrilla presidential campaigns in 1984 and 1988: as it turned out, this aide who came latest to King, and was perhaps most mistrusted by him, would come closest to developing into his heir as the single most eloquent symbol of pride and hope for masses of black Americans. Andrew Young, in his customary diligent and thoughtful manner, respectably worked his way on to become a Georgia congressman, Jimmy Carter's U.S. delegate to the United Nations, mayor of Atlanta. But James Bevel, the most mystically intense of King's attendants, "just sort of could never find a home after King died," says Young, and he was to wander in time into an improbable involvement with Lyndon LaRouche's esoteric society of ultrareactionary zealots. Abernathy's case was even more melancholy. Having abided since those first days in Montgomery as King's closest friend, with King now gone, he steadily receded into a rather dowdy obscurity, climaxed by the ignominy, to King's other old aides and most black leaders, of his baldly opportunistic support for Ronald Reagan's presidential candidacy in 1980, after which he found himself nonetheless briskly discarded by the Reagan administration.

Meanwhile, sorrow did not quit King's family. Eighteen months after his assassination, his long-troubled younger brother, A.D., having been called back to replace King as co-pastor with their father at Ebenezer, was found one morning drowned in the swimming pool of his home. Five years later, King's mother, Alberta, was playing the organ as usual at the Sunday morning service at Ebenezer when a deranged black youth in the congregation arose and shot her to death. But Daddy King — so blasted again and again — yet endured: his sturdy, chestily stern figure became a familiar fixture at Democratic conventions, civil rights rallies, the unending commemorations of his oldest son's life and death, until, on a Sunday in the autumn of 1984, after returning from the morning worship service at Ebenezer and sitting down to dinner with the remains of his family, he died of a heart attack.

He had passed the years since Memphis joined in a religious attendance to King's memory with Coretta, who had translated herself into a kind of madonna-like icon, a calm, grave effigy herself of mourning and remembrance. She would later relate that, about three weeks before Memphis, King had surprised her by presenting her with an arrangement of red carnations that, when she touched them, she realized were artificial: "I wanted to give you something that you could always keep," she reported King told her. She would also indicate in later years that, on what turned out to be their last night together before he left again for Memphis, she had led him upstairs to their bedroom and given him all the solace and love left to her to give. Now, long after the funeral that brilliant and mufflingly hot April day in the plain brick edifice of Ebenezer, among the filling stations and cafés and nightspots of Auburn Avenue where King had preached for eight years — the sanctuary packed that Tuesday morning with senators, congressmen, the attorney general, the vice president of the United States, Jacqueline Kennedy — long after their departure, through the months that followed it was as if the funeral still went on from Sunday to Sunday around her, the hymning and unceasing elegies still grieving for him, heads dropping and handkerchiefs wiping eyes in the congregation to which he had confided his spirit's anguishings over the years. And she sat in the same pew near the front, her face lifted slightly with its graven, masklike composure as she listened to Daddy King cry out from the pulpit in a shivering voice, "It was the *hate* in this land that took my son away from me. . . ."

There has continued to linger like a low, dim fever the speculation that not just James Earl Ray — the chronic petty criminal from the scruffiest and most rabid outskirts of American racism, who was eventually convicted of King's assassination — but some wider conspiracy had to be accountable for what happened in Memphis, a conjecture advanced to a certitude in later years by King's family, especially vigorously by his grown children. But singular figures like King, who seem somehow to quicken the nerves of society's sense of life and possibilities, who open up a nation's collective experience to such unaccustomed excitements and portents, also immediately attract ambush. And much of the urge to believe that King had to have been slain by a conspiracy arises — as in the deaths of the two Kennedy brothers — from a reluctance to accept the maddeningly absurd disparity that so much could have been effaced through so paltry an agent acting only out of his own dingy and solitary deliriums: it seem to violate some natural symmetry. But life has never particularly proceeded according to geometrically rational equilibriums. And one should always be wary of explanations — including, in King's case, despite the malevolence of J. Edgar Hoover, any actual complicity by the FBI — that ultimately wind up more baroque than the paradoxes they are trying to explain. At the same time, given the pattern of Hoover's mounting abhorrence of King, neither should one dismiss yet the question of what he might have known about what was afoot in Memphis but simply chose not to act on.

But by Memphis, many have since maintained, King's movement had already begun to dissipate anyway, passing into the sporadic and inconclusive skirmishes — over busing, affirmative action, the delinquencies of government social programs, all occupied not so much with revolutionizing the heart of the nation as with reengineering policy and administrative procedures — that were to characterize the dwindled decades after him. Those lesser and distracted times inevitably raised the question, though, of whether a catalytic folk figure is not, despite the old Tolstoy argument, in fact indispensable to any movement that will be wide and passionate enough to effect a social transformation as profound as that which King brought to pass at least in the South.

But some have since suggested that it was just at the point where King seemed passing irretrievably into decline that he came by the terrible exaltation of violent martyrdom — a kind of historical editing, before the disillusionment could become total, that spared him from what could well have become a progressive marginality and tiresomeness and bankruptcy of his image. The Reverend Samuel Kyles, with King on the balcony when he was shot, reflects now: "People wear leaders out. If you do fifteen years, you're doing good. I tell you, if Martin had lived to be sixty-five, there'd never have been a holiday in his honor, because we would've used him up. Had he lived, he'd walk into a room now and we'd say, 'Oh, there's Dr. King. Hey, Martin, have a seat.' 'Cause life is like that, you know." Even as it is, King's own family members have since collaborated with certain other interests in a dismal trivialization of his memory, by not only personally syndicating him, despite his immense historical resonance, as their own patented, copyrighted property, exacting fees for the use of his image and words, but lending their license, for considerations accordingly, to such stupendous banalizations of his meaning as the exploitation of his great moment at the Washington March for an Internet company television commercial. But if King had lived, most likely he would, with his increasingly radical gospel, have departed steadily further from the temper and received liberal sophistications of his times, drifting to the outermost fringes of apparent relevancy — to the final true desert of the prophet, in a reverse of the scriptural sequence going back, as it were, to John the Baptist.

It will probably forever remain the irony, though, that it is not for where he finally wound up, but for his beginnings that he is commemorated and revered.

Finally, I remember a memorial march,

about a month after Memphis, that surged through a black neighborhood in Washington that still had a scorched and bombed-out look from the rage and flames that had erupted there after King's slaying. But this was an eclectic accumulation of citizens, black and white and brown, priests and militants and students, that was curiously like some stray atmospheric reflection in time of Selma, King's last true great moment — all of them moving, eerily voiceless, in a flickering of rain, past rubbled lots and broken, roofless walls and empty windows through which one could glimpse the low, smoky sky. Near the front of the march was a limousine bearing Coretta, the crowd milling around it to get some glimpse of her, the heat from its engine breath-smothering in the rain, but she was lost to them behind the dark-tinted windows. . . . Presently, however, a singing began to gather up and down the length of the procession, a rising, ghostlike choiring and clapping of those huge anthems of all the marches and mass meetings from that simpler, heroic time of Montgomery and Birmingham and Selma, which had the sound now almost of some incantatory labor to call him forth again. Then, briefly, the sun broke through the rain — a point-blank unrelenting Southern sun — under which the steaming streets shone with a soft silver light: and for an instant his presence did seem actually to be there — he *had* to be somewhere in the midst of that procession and that singing, it would only be a second before one would see him again, that stocky figure striding along in his shirtsleeves with a calm gaze on his round, bland face of a solitary and infinitely patient purpose, some removed and inner communion even in the midst of that throng with cosmic reaches, and despite everything still trying, if nothing else he never did know how to cease *trying*. But that sense of his imminent appearance was there only for an instant, as brief as a single indrawing and release of breath, and what returned was the awareness — which has lasted through all these years since — of an enormous, immeasurable absence.

Note

A vast wilderness of writing about King has proliferated over the years since Montgomery and Memphis, ranging from the worshipful to the perfunctory to the respectably perceptive to, now and then, the inspired. For this account, I have particularly mined from the reportage in several biographies. David Garrow's *Bearing the Cross*, which appeared in 1986, is a formidably compendious, if somewhat uninflected and metronomic, logging of King's almost weekly progress from Montgomery up to the instant of his death. One of the early, more intellectually ambitious reviews of King's ministry, though a bit cursory in narrative particulars and at times a touch professorially overly exegetical, is David Levering Lewis's *King*, the second edition appearing in 1978. In 1983, Stephen Oates produced a rather reverential but worthily diligent biography, *Let the Trumpet Sound*.

But nothing so far has matched, in fully bodied, dramatic sweep of story, Taylor Branch's magisterial *America in the King Years* — especially the first volume, in 1988,

Parting the Waters. Its mighty narrative surge tends to lose its way, in the second volume, *Pillar of Fire*, in the complicating thickets of the general American experience. But both are monumental as chronicles of the soul struggle and folk pageantry of the great Black Awakening and King's own agonies and splendors during that time.

Also of value in this review of King's life:

Abernathy, Ralph David. *And the Walls Came Tumbling Down*. New York: Harper & Row, 1989.

Ansbro, John J. *Martin Luther King, Jr.: The Making of a Mind*. Maryknoll, N.Y.: Orbis Books, 1982.

Cone, James H. *Martin & Malcolm & America: A Dream or a Nightmare*. Maryknoll, N.Y.: Orbis Books, 1991.

Dyson, Michael Eric. *I May Not Get There with You: The True Story of Martin Luther King, Jr.* New York.: The Free Press, 2000.

Frank, Gerold. *An American Death*. Garden City, N.Y.: Doubleday, 1972.

Garrow, David J. *The FBI and Martin Luther King, Jr.* New York: Penguin Books, 1981.

Goldman, Peter. *The Death and Life of*

Malcolm X. Urbana and Chicago: University of Illinois Press, 1979.

Huie, William Bradford. *He Slew the Dreamer*. New York: Delacorte Press, 1970.

King, Coretta Scott. *My Life with Martin Luther King, Jr.* New York: Holt, Rinehart, and Winston, 1969.

Lewis, John, with Michael D'Orso. *Walking with the Wind: A Memoir of the Movement*. New York: Simon & Schuster, 1998.

Reeves, Richard. *President Kennedy: Profile of Power*. New York: Simon & Schuster, 1993.

Viorst, Milton. *Fire in the Streets: America in the 1960s*. New York: Simon & Schuster, 1979.

Weisberg, Harold. *Frame-Up: The Martin Luther King–James Earl Ray Case*. New York: Outerbridge & Dienstfrey, 1971.

Young, Andrew. *A Way Out of No Way: The Spiritual Memoirs of Andrew Young*. Nashville: Thomas Nelson, 1994.

Finally, I must acknowledge my great appreciation for the special assistance lent to the backgrounding of this story by the deft enterprise of Katrina Maestri.